"In *Meet Generation Z* James Emery White shares helpful insights into the generation that follows the Millennial generation in a clear, practical way. Pastors and church leaders seeking to better understand the world of their youth ought to read this text."

Ed Stetzer, Billy Graham Distinguished Chair, Wheaton College

"*Meet Generation Z* is much more than just another popular sociological interpretation of our current cultural moment, as important as such an analysis, in and of itself, may be. This new and outstanding work by James Emery White, characteristic of the excellence we have come to expect from his prolific publications, provides not only wise and thoughtful cultural interpretation but also important theological insight regarding the trends, ideas, and movements that have shaped our twenty-first-century world. Christian leaders who are not only serious about church and ministry but who also want to understand and engage culture in order to connect this post-Christian world with the claims of the gospel will find White's work to be essential reading. Highly recommended!"

David S. Dockery, president, Trinity International University/
Trinity Evangelical Divinity School

"It's clear that Jim has a white-hot passion for Generation Z to know God. His research, practical applications, and desire for all church leaders to get this right will inspire and challenge you."

Sue Miller, children's ministry champion;
Orange Conference staff;
coauthor of *Not Normal: 7 Quirks
of Incredible Volunteers*

MEET GENERATION

MEET GENERATION

Z

UNDERSTANDING AND REACHING THE NEW POST-CHRISTIAN WORLD

JAMES EMERY WHITE

BakerBooks

a division of Baker Publishing Group
Grand Rapids, Michigan

Published by Baker Books
a division of Baker Publishing Group
P.O. Box 6287, Grand Rapids, MI 49516-6287
www.bakerbooks.com

Printed in the United States of America

Library of Congress Cataloging-in-Publication Data
Names: White, James Emery, 1961– author.
Title: Meet generation Z : understanding and reaching the new post-Christian world / James Emery White.
Description: Grand Rapids : Baker Books, 2017. | Includes bibliographical references.
Identifiers: LCCN 2016033232 | ISBN 9780801017018 (pbk.)
Subjects: LCSH: Non-church-affiliated people. | Evangelistic work.
Classification: LCC BV4921.3 .W445 2017 | DDC 269/.2—dc23
LC record available at https://lccn.loc.gov/2016033232

17 18 19 20 21 22 23   7 6 5 4

Contents

Contents

Acknowledgments

I wish to thank the Baker team for its support of this project, our sixth together, and specifically Bob Hosack, who was a strong advocate for this book from the moment of its conception.

Alli Main continues to earn my deepest gratitude for her assistance with all of my writing. Whether through research or editing, feedback or ideas, she is nothing less than a godsend. Grayson Pope helped weigh in on study questions and also gave good advice on needed additions to the book as a whole. And as always, my wife, Susan, continues to make every page possible.

Finally, to Mecklenburg Community Church, an amazing community of people who continue to die to themselves daily in countless ways in order to reach out to their friends and family, neighbors and coworkers with the message of Christ. It's an honor to be your pastor.

I will teach you hidden lessons from our past—
    stories we have heard and known,
    stories our ancestors handed down to us.
We will not hide these truths from our children;
    we will tell the next generation
about the glorious deeds of the LORD,
    about his power and his mighty wonders.
For he issued his laws to Jacob;
    he gave his instructions to Israel.
He commanded our ancestors
    to teach them to their children,
so the next generation might know them—
    even the children not yet born—
    and they in turn will teach their own children.
So each generation should set its hope anew on God,
    not forgetting his glorious miracles
    and obeying his commands.

Psalm 78:2–7 NLT

Introduction

They are the Final Generation.

Gen Z 2025 Report

This is not another pop-sociological book about a particular generation. This is a book about the most significant cultural challenge facing the Western church that just so happens to be reflected in a new generation.

A recent survey of thirty-five thousand Americans by the Pew Research Center found that the rise of the "nones" has grown to encompass 23 percent of America's adults. This means that nearly one out of every four adults in the United States, when asked about their religious identity, would say "nothing." Further, many who were once in the church are now leaving it. About 19 percent of Americans would call themselves "former" Christians.

The generation being shaped most significantly by this, often called Generation Z, will come to typify the new reality of a post-Christian world. As the first truly post-Christian generation, and numerically the largest, Generation Z will be the most influential religious force in the West and the heart of the missional challenge facing the Christian church.

Unfortunately, the realities of a post-Christian context for the West have yet to be fully grasped by the Western church, much less responded to. Yet the rise of the nones and the coming force of Generation Z will inevitably challenge every church to rethink its strategy in light of a cultural landscape that has shifted seismically. If the heart of the Christian mission is to evangelize and transform culture through the centrality of the church, then understanding that culture is paramount. It is toward that end this work is offered as a hopeful complement to my earlier works: *Serious Times* and *The Rise of the Nones*.

This book has two parts. The first details the new realities facing the Christian church. Chapter 1 explores what I call the second fall and the rise of the nones, including the latest research on the new post-Christian realities facing the West. This sets the context for the world Generation Z both inhabits and is being shaped by. The second chapter is an introduction to Generation Z—what marks them and defines them. A third chapter is offered on the specific family context that is shaping them in ways unlike any other generation in history.

The second part turns the corner toward response, including the importance of truly becoming countercultural as a church. This is followed with a look at how to speak into the culture we are countering in ways that are both winsome and compelling. The final chapters explore new approaches to evangelism and apologetics, as well as the strategic decisions the church I pastor has made to reach the unchurched and Generation Z.

Finally, I've provided three appendices featuring three talks I delivered at Mecklenburg Community Church (Meck) that reflect issues relevant to reaching Generation Z. The first is an example of how to address a controversial issue—in this case, gay marriage. The second explores the world of the occult (and our culture's fascination with it) by mapping out the spiritual world. And the third is an example of how one might build an apologetic bridge for the sake of pre-evangelism using science.

This book, as with others I've written, is not simply theory or even research. Meck, which I have had the privilege of leading for nearly three decades, experiences over 70 percent of its growth from the unchurched. Demographically, we have skewed younger every year for the last decade. Reaching the emerging, post-Christian generation is not rhetoric for us but the reality that consumes us daily. It is my hope and prayer that this book serves countless other churches on the same path.

PART 1

THE NEW REALITY

1

A Seventh Age, the Second Fall, and the Rise of the Nones

Religion is the key of history.

Lord Acton

A Seventh Age

One of the more intriguing observations about the flow of history surfaced in an important essay written just after the Second World War that I was introduced to while studying at Oxford University in England. It was written by a historian named Christopher Dawson. In it he makes the case that there have been six identifiable "ages" in relation to the Christian church and faith, each lasting for three or four centuries and each following a similar course: each of these ages began and then ended in crisis.

The heart of each crisis was the same: intense attack by new enemies from within and from outside the church, which in turn demanded new spiritual determination and drive. Without this determination and drive, the church would have lost the day. Dawson accounted for six such ages at the time of his writing.[1] I believe we are now living at the start of another. We are at the end of an age and stand at the beginning of another.

A seventh age.

I am not alone in sensing we live in a pivotal time. Political strategist Doug Sosnik is famed in Washington circles for his "closely held, big-think memos on the state of American politics." He believes the United States is "going through the most significant period of change since the beginning of the Industrial Revolution." Years from now, Sosnik argues, "we are going to look back at this period of time and see it as a 'hinge' moment . . . a connection point that ties two historical periods in time, one before and one afterwards."[2]

Identifying these "hinge moments" is actually a deeply biblical idea. The Bible lauds the men of Issachar for being sensitive to exactly these kinds of dynamics: "From the tribe of Issachar, there were 200 leaders. . . . All these men understood the signs of the times and knew the best course for Israel to take" (1 Chron. 12:32 NLT). That tandem—knowing the signs of the times *and* how best to live in light of them—is key.

So what signs are going to mark this seventh age? Few are unaware of the economic uncertainty, global instability, technological advances, and demographic transitions that abound. But what specifically are the trends, the patterns, the movements, and most of all, in relation to Dawson's thesis, the crises from within and from without the church that we should pay attention to?

There are quite a few from which to choose.

From within the Christian movement itself, there is the expansion of Christianity southward in Africa, Asia, and Latin America that can only be called explosive. And with it, the new challenge of the globalization of Christianity. Philip Jenkins argues that by the year 2050 only one Christian out of five will be a non-Latino white person, and the center of gravity of the Christian world will have shifted firmly to the Southern Hemisphere.[3] The challenges this will bring are enormous, including the relationship between the Western and the non-Western church, which has not always been an easy one.

Another significant challenge is the continued rise of Islam and whether Islam will modernize peacefully or we will continue to have what Samuel Huntington presciently called the clash of civilizations that has so defined our world since 9/11.[4] In other words, will the future of Islam be the model of, say, Indonesia or that of ISIS? Of equal global importance is what will lead China once Marxism falls. Will it be some form of continued authoritarianism, a national socialism, a type of Buddhism, or the surfacing of the underground Christian church?

Another major crisis to be reckoned with on a different front is the radical redefinition of the most foundational institutions within creation itself—marriage and family. No longer is family defined as a male husband and a female wife, much less involving children. Male with male, female with female, children with surrogates, multiple parents, polygamy, and polyamorous unions abound. In 2015, Britain became the first country in the world to allow three-parent babies.[5] It is a new day in which the very idea of family is being recast in light of personal desire.

But even beyond family is the challenge brought to the very idea of what it means to be human. I have long told my graduate theology students that the doctrine of humanity is, by far, the most pressing doctrine of our day in regard to culture. It is the one area of Christian thought that is most challenged by the world in which we live, not to mention the one we have the least to draw from historically. Find a reflection from Origen or Athanasius,

Luther or Melanchthon, Barth or Brunner that speaks to stem-cell research, human cloning, or transsexualism. As the first five centuries hammered out Christology and later generations tackled everything from the Holy Spirit to revelation, ours is the generation that will be forced to examine and elucidate the doctrine of humanity in ways that confront both changing morals and new technological frontiers.

The Second Fall

But the most profound cultural challenge is the one that encompasses all of these trends and more. *It's the cultural context itself.* And what is that cultural context? The great crisis of this seventh age is that there has been a second fall. The first fall led to God's expulsion of human beings from the Garden of Eden. The second fall was when we returned the favor. In our world, increasing numbers of people lead their lives without any sense of needing to look to a higher power, to something outside of themselves. Leaders of science and commerce, education and politics—regardless of their personal views—do not tend to operate with any reference to a transcendent truth, much less a God.

At first glance, you may not think this has really happened, particularly in the United States. Most people in the United States believe in God. It could be argued, as Peter Berger once did, that America is "as furiously religious as it ever was, and in some places more so than ever."[6] But something like atheism isn't at the heart of the second fall, because philosophical atheism is not at the heart of secularism nor the principal challenge to Christian faith.

The heart of secularism is a *functional* atheism. Rather than rejecting the idea of God, our culture simply ignores him. Or as Cathy Lynn Grossman, the co-researcher of the famed 2008 American Religious Identification Survey documenting the rise of the nones, concluded, people today "aren't [merely] secularized. They're not thinking about religion and rejecting it; they're not thinking about it at all."[7]

This is a new and profound break with the history of Western thought and culture. Even among those times and places that might be called pagan, true secularity in this sense was unknown. Whether it was the God of Abraham, Isaac, and Jacob or the gods of Greece and Rome, there were gods—something outside of themselves that people looked to. It would have been alien to anyone's thinking to begin and end with themselves *alone* in terms of truth and morality, which means there would never have been a sense in which such things were self-generated or self-determined. No more. The second fall changed all of that and now shapes the world in which we live.

Specifically, for the West, this means we live in a world that is post-Christian. And it also explains why we now talk about the rise of the nones.

The Rise of the Nones

So who are the nones? The short answer is that they are the religiously unaffiliated. When asked about their religion on various surveys and polls, they do not answer "Baptist" or "Catholic" or any other defined faith. They simply say, "I'm nothing."

And their numbers are rising. Faster than any other group.

At the time I completed my book *The Rise of the Nones*, the nones made up one out of every five Americans, which made them the second largest religious group in the United States—second only to Catholics. They were also the fastest-growing religious group in the nation. And when I wrote about their growth being fast, I meant fast (see fig. 1.1).

The number of nones in the 1930s and 1940s hovered around 5 percent. By 1990, that number had risen to only 8.1 percent, a mere

Figure 1.1
Percentage of Americans Claiming No Religious Identity

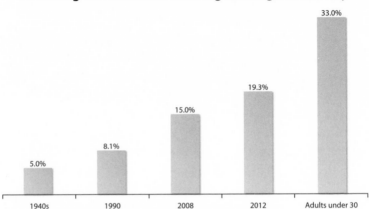

3 percent rise in over half a century. Between 1990 and 2008—just eighteen years—the number of nones nearly doubled, jumping from 8.1 percent to 15 percent. Then in just four short years, it climbed to nearly 20 percent, representing one out of every five Americans. And for adults under the age of thirty, it increased to one out of every three people.[8]

But it's gotten worse.

The latest figures from the General Social Survey were released in 2015, filling in the gap between 2012 and 2014. This was followed by findings released from the Pew Research Center based on its massive US Religious Landscape Study. In just two years, the nones climbed from 19 percent to 23 percent, or nearly one out of every four adults (see fig. 1.2).

The nones are no longer the second largest religious group in the United States; they are the largest.[9] And they are still, by far, the fastest growing. But the significance is not simply that the nones are growing; the number of professing Christians is also shrinking. The percentage of adults who described themselves as Christian in 2014 dropped nearly nine percentage points from the previous Pew study in 2007. So now only about 71 percent

Figure 1.2

Percentage of Americans Claiming No Religious Identity

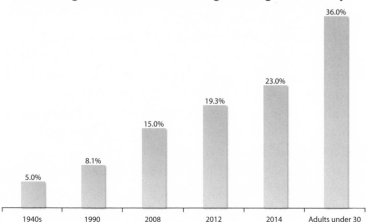

of American adults would call themselves Christian, down from nearly 80 percent.

More troubling is that of the 85 percent of American adults who were raised Christian, nearly a quarter of them no longer identify with Christianity. Former Christians now represent 19.2 percent of the US adult population overall. To put this into perspective, says Allen Cooperman, Pew's director of religion research, "There are more than four former Christians for every convert to Christianity."[10] And the rise of the nones and the fall of Christians is widespread, crossing race, gender, educational, and geographic barriers. Forget the Bible Belt or the Catholic North. This is happening everywhere and across every demographic.[11]

Another dynamic is that with each passing year the self-described nones are growing more secular. In a 2015 release of additional data from its 2014 Religious Landscape Study, the Pew Research Center found that over the last seven years, the number of nones who continue to believe in God or pray daily was in ongoing decline; 62 percent never pray and 33.3 percent do not believe in God. In 2007, 57 percent of all nones felt religion was of little importance to their lives; in 2014, that number climbed to roughly two-thirds of all respondents. So there is not only a growth of the nones but also a growing secularism within their ranks. Even those who believe in God, who at 89 percent of all US adults remain the overwhelming majority, are wavering in that belief. Of the 89 percent who believe God exists, only 63 percent say they are "absolutely certain" of that existence.

This constitutes a significant change from earlier observations indicating that while the nones were growing, their spirituality was not waning. This was an encouraging dynamic in the face of growing religious disaffection. That encouraging dynamic is no longer in play.

The situation is even worse in regard to younger respondents (see table below). While 33 percent of what Pew calls "older Millennials" are among the nones, that number climbs to 36 percent of what it calls "younger Millennials."[12] Beyond self-classification of religious identity, there is also a marked difference with age in terms of religious belief and practice. For example, among Baby Boomers, six out of ten say they pray every day. Only four out of ten of the youngest Millennials would concur. And, Pew reports, they do not seem to be growing more religiously observant as they get older. On the contrary, the oldest Millennials, now in their late twenties and early thirties, are generally less observant than when they were surveyed seven years earlier.[13]

The same results have been found through other research projects. Barna Group has concluded, based on fifteen metrics related to faith, that nearly half of the nation's adult population (44 percent) now qualifies as post-Christian.[14] But that's not all. "The pattern is indisputable: The younger the generation, the more post-Christian it is."[15]

So where have the nones gone? Nowhere. That's the point. There is no shift from Christianity to another religious brand. Instead, there is simply the abandonment of a defined religion altogether.

In Many Ways, Younger Americans
Are Less Religious Than Older Americans

Percent of US adults who say . . .

	Silent Genera-tion (born 1928–45)	Baby Boom-ers (born 1946–64)	Gen-eration X (born 1965–80)	Older Millenni-als (born 1981–89)	Younger Millenni-als (born 1990–96)
Religious Behaviors					
They pray daily	67	61	56	46	39
They attend services at least weekly	51	38	34	27	28
Religious Beliefs					
They believe in God	92	92	89	84	80
With absolute certainty	71	69	64	54	50
They believe in heaven	75	74	72	67	68
They believe Scrip-ture is the Word of God	69	64	61	50	52
They believe in hell	57	59	59	55	56
Religion's Importance					
Religion is very important in their lives	67	59	53	44	38

Source: 2014 Religious Landscape Study, conducted June 4–September 30, 2014, Pew Research Center.

Those who used to be simply "unchurched" are now dropping out completely.

What has this meant for the life of the church? It's not pretty. Figure 1.3 graphs the last twenty years in regard to church attendance alone.

In 1994, 62 percent of Americans attended a church frequently. In 2013, barely half attended more than seldom or never. The same is true when plotting church membership, religion's importance in

Figure 1.3
Decline of Church Attendance

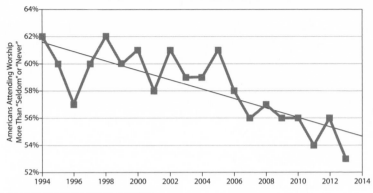

Graph by *Corner of Church and State*, an RNS blog.
Source: Gallup.

life, and religion's relevance to today. All are in free fall. Combining all such graphs into one, the Religion News Service put together a graph titled "The Great Decline" (see fig. 1.4).[16]

This situation is not unique to the American scene. According to the latest data from the first stage of the 2015 British Election Study, a survey of more than twenty thousand people by a team

Figure 1.4
The Great Decline: Average of Five Gallup Measures

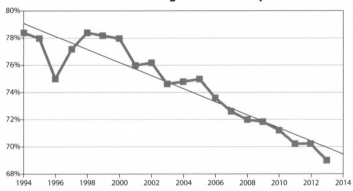

Graph by *Corner of Church and State*, an RNS blog.
Source: Gallup.

Figure 1.5
Percentage of Nones in the United Kingdom

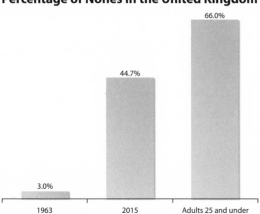

of academics from Manchester, Oxford, and Nottingham Universities, the nones in the United Kingdom have risen from just 3 percent in 1963 to 44.7 percent today—a stunning rise for just five decades (see fig. 1.5). And among adults age twenty-five and under, the number of nones climbed to nearly two-thirds.[17]

So pronounced is this trend in the UK that a two-year commission, involving leading religious leaders from all faiths, has called for public life in Britain to be "systematically de-Christianised." In other words, Britain is no longer a Christian country and should stop acting as if it is.[18]

So is the Christian sky falling? Many cultural observers have countered the dismal statistics with the following truths—and they are true:

- Christianity is on the rise worldwide, particularly in the global South.
- Christianity remains the world's largest faith, and the most distant projections to 2050 see it maintaining that lead (this includes the United States, with 71 percent currently affirming a Christian faith).[19]

So it would certainly be correct to say that rumors of Christianity's death are premature. Yet any informed observer also knows the following:

- The rise of the nones throughout the West is real and cannot be ignored.
- The "squishy center" is being pushed away from Christianity and, as a result, is rapidly changing the American cultural landscape.

Did the last one leave you a bit puzzled? It's worth exploring, because it is the essence of the answer to one of the more important questions surrounding this entire conversation; namely, "What is driving all this?"

The Squishy Center

When it comes to driving forces in relation to such things as the rise of the nones, most would say it's happening because we now live in a post-Christian world. The thinking is that processes such as secularization, privatization, and pluralization have taken their inevitable toll.

That is true. And it is critical we understand all three processes.

Secularization is the process by which something *becomes* secular. It is the cultural current making things secular. Famed sociologist Peter Berger defined secularization as the process by which "sectors of society and culture are removed from the domination of religious institutions and symbols."[20] This simply means that the church is losing its influence as a shaper of life and thought in the wider social order, and Christianity is losing its place as the dominant worldview.

Privatization is the process by which a chasm is created between the public and the private spheres of life, and spiritual things are increasingly placed within the private arena.[21] So when it comes to things such as business, politics, or even marriage and the home, personal faith is bracketed off.

Pluralization is the process by which individuals are confronted with a staggering number of ideologies and faith options competing for their attention.[22] The number of options for the private sphere to consider multiplies explosively, but particularly at the level of worldview and faith.[23] Peter Berger speaks of the traditional role of religion as a "sacred canopy" covering the contemporary culture. Religion, at least in terms of the idea of there being a God that life and thought have to consider, once blanketed all of society and culture. Today that canopy is gone, replaced instead by millions of small tents under which we can choose to dwell.[24]

Think about the effect of these cultural currents. Secularization means there is less of a supportive context for faith. Privatization has made all things related to faith a private affair, like having a favorite color or food. But most devastating of all has been pluralization. Not only are there multiple faiths and worldviews contending for our attention, but there is also the idea that they are all equally valid, equally true.

Yet the real power of these forces is their effect on what I call the "squishy center."

Let's set up a couple of extremes. In figure 1.6 I've set on one end the hard-core secularists and estimated them at 25 percent of the country. That might be generous, but it makes for easy math to demonstrate the cultural dynamic at play.

Figure 1.6

Secularists
25%

On the other end (see fig. 1.7) are the true believers. These are individuals who have come to faith in Christ, and he operates as their Forgiver and Leader, emphasis on the "Leader" part. These people are not Christian in name only but have had the deepest needs of their lives intersected by Christ, and their relationship with him is changing them to reflect him more with each passing year. Let's make them 25 percent too, which also might be generous.

Figure 1.7

Secularists	Believers
25%	25%

These two poles are not without warrant. The latest findings from Pew's American Religious Landscape Study found that not only are the nones growing more secular, but the truly religious are also growing more devout.[25]

In between these two poles, we have 50 percent of the country. This is the squishy center (see fig. 1.8). And it is squishy because those in its midst tend to be soft and pliable in terms of being shaped. Their individual beliefs have little definition, and even less conviction. If they consider themselves Christian, it is with a small *c*. Those in the center do not have the solidity of the secularist or the believer. As a result, those in the center tend to move toward whatever is culturally most influencing. However the culture tends to mold, shape, and pressure is how they are molded, shaped, and pressured.

Figure 1.8

Secularists	Squishy Center	Believers
25%	50%	25%

In the past, the forces within culture tended to move the center toward the believers' side of things. This meant that those hovering in the squishy center, if asked, would have said they were a Christian. That was the cultural thing to say. And they probably would have gone to church—at least on special days. There was cultural pressure on them if they didn't.

But culture has changed. It's not moving people that way anymore. It's not shaping people that way anymore. Now virtually everything in culture is moving the squishy center to the secularists' side. Today, if asked about their religion, people in the center say they're nothing, because that's the cultural thing to say. And they don't go to church, because that's also the cultural thing *not* to do. This is what I mean by the squishy center and the way culture dictates to it.

Even modern representations of bygone eras when culture moved the squishy center to the Christian side of things airbrush such realities away. For example, look at the enormously popular BBC show *Downton Abbey*. When asked why the series failed to show Christianity as a central part of the characters' lives (which would have been the norm for aristocracy in the early part of the twentieth century), the show's historical consultant gave a blunt answer. The executives in charge of the series ordered producers to "leave religion out of it" for fear of alienating an increasingly atheistic public. As a result, the Crawley family is never shown in the process of sitting down at the table for dinner; instead, the action begins partway through the meal—all to avoid having to show the characters saying grace, which they very much would have done.[26]

Few cultural observers within the Christian community deny this dynamic in regard to culture and the squishy center. However, there are varied responses. The most prevalent is to use it to try to calm everyone down in regard to the rise of the nones and other troubling headlines. After all, the thinking goes, we're just losing the "nominals." And a little sloughing off of the uncommitted fringe, it is maintained, can be a good thing. And further, they would add, it's not like we "lost" someone who was truly "found." So the idea being promoted is, "Don't worry; it's not a big deal."

I take a different view. I would argue that it is a *very* big deal. The nominal population, no matter how it was shaped historically, has always been America's mission field. It's who Wesley and Whitefield, Moody and Graham won to Christ. The squishy center has always been the prime evangelistic target. Its inhabitants were the ones most open, the ones who represented the fields white unto harvest.

We must realize, as the old saying goes, that "facts are our friends," meaning that reality, no matter how much it bites, is always worth biting into. The important news of late is that reaching the nominals has become a much tougher task. So rather than heave a huge sigh of relief that evangelical faith may not be losing any ground in terms of percentage points, we must recognize that all this means is that we are, for now, holding our own.

But "holding our own" isn't exactly the mission.

Perhaps even more alarming is that as the squishy center moves increasingly toward the secular side of things, swelling the ranks of the nones, the bridge those very nominals once offered between the two sides of believers and secularists is fast disappearing. As Ed Stetzer has rightly observed, "In the past, those of nominal faith were a bridge between the Christian community and the irreligious community. As the cultural cost of being a Christian increases, people who were once Christian in name only likely have started to identify as nones, disintegrating the 'ideological bridge' between unbelievers and believers."[27]

But this is about more than losing an ideological bridge. We are also losing a relational bridge—one we can walk across to reach the largest generation in American history.

Discussion Questions

1. Do you sense that we are about to enter a seventh age, as you read about earlier? What are a few of the trends you see going on around you or mentioned in this chapter that make you feel this way?

2. Why is the doctrine of humanity the most pressing doctrine of our day?

3. As a result of the second fall, our culture is not rejecting the idea of God but rather simply ignoring him. What is the difference between ignoring God and outright rejecting him?

4. The nones are now the largest religious group in America, accounting for one out of every four adults. Not only that, but for every convert to Christianity, there are more than four former Christians. Do you recognize the size of the nones as a group and the religious shift that is happening in the population? Is your church's ministry reflective of these changes?

5. These days barely half of Americans attend church more than seldom or never. Does your service planning take this into account? If not, how could it?

6. Why is it a big deal that the United States is losing the largely nominal population of believers (the squishy center)?

2

Meet Generation Z

One generation passeth away, and another generation cometh.

Ecclesiastes 1:4 KJV

Each year students begin college across the nation, forming a new freshman class. In the spirit of understanding generational change, the good folk at Beloit College produce an annual college freshman mindset list. Consider one of their more recent, based on the 2015 freshman class. Students heading into their first year of college in 2015 were mostly eighteen and were born in 1997.

Here are a few of Beloit's observations:

- Among those who were not alive in their lifetimes are Princess Diana, Notorious B.I.G., Jacques Cousteau, and Mother Teresa.
- Joining them in the world the year they were born were Dolly the sheep, the McCaughey septuplets, and Michael "Prince" Jackson Jr.

Since they have been on the planet:

- Hybrid automobiles have always been mass produced.
- Google has always existed, in its founding words, "to organize the world's information and make it universally accessible."
- They have never licked a postage stamp.
- Email has become the new "formal" communication, while texts and tweets remain enclaves for the casual.
- Four foul-mouthed kids have always been playing in South Park.
- Hong Kong has always been under Chinese rule.
- They have grown up treating Wi-Fi as an entitlement.
- The announcement of someone being the first woman to hold a position has impressed only their parents.
- Charlton Heston is recognized for waving a rifle over his head as much as for waving his staff over the Red Sea.
- Cell phones have become so ubiquitous in class that teachers don't know which students are using them to take notes and which ones are planning a party.
- If you say, "Around the turn of the century," they may well ask you, "Which one?"
- They avidly joined Harry Potter, Ron, and Hermione as they built their reading skills through all seven volumes.
- Attempts at human cloning have never been federally funded but do require FDA approval.
- The therapeutic use of marijuana has always been legal in a growing number of American states.
- Teachers have always had to insist that term papers employ sources in addition to those found online.
- *The Lion King* has always been on Broadway.
- At least Mom and Dad had their new Nintendo 64 to help them get through long nights sitting up with the baby.

- First responders have always been heroes.
- Splenda has always been a sweet option in the United States.
- The Atlanta Braves have always played at Turner Field.
- Proud parents recorded their first steps on camcorders mounted on their shoulders like bazookas.
- They have had no idea how fortunate they were to enjoy the final four years of federal budget surpluses.[1]

There is one other mark, of course. One that is, without a doubt, the most significant. One that the Beloit observers neglected to include.

The freshman class of 2015 embodies an entirely new generation: Generation Z.

Generation Z

I know some are still trying to catch up with Busters, or Generation X, or whatever we called whoever followed the Boomers. Or maybe you leapfrogged over all that straight to Generation Y (Millennials), on whom marketers have been focused for at least a decade. I could tell you there are actually six living generations in America, but I don't want to add to your stress.[2]

Let me save you some time. Drop everything and start paying attention to Generation Z, which now constitutes 25.9 percent of the US population (see fig. 2.1). That's more than Millennials (24.5 percent). That's more than Gen X (15.4 percent). Yes, that's even more than Baby Boomers (23.6 percent).[3] By 2020, members of Generation Z will account for 40 percent of all consumers.[4] They will not simply influence American culture, as any generation would; they will constitute American culture.

So who falls into Generation Z? There's still some debate on exact dates, but essentially it involves those who were born after

Figure 2.1

Percentage of Population by Generation

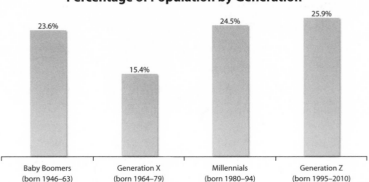

Baby Boomers	Generation X	Millennials	Generation Z
(born 1946–63)	(born 1964–79)	(born 1980–94)	(born 1995–2010)
23.6%	15.4%	24.5%	25.9%

Generation Y, so approximately 1995 to around 2010. It is the generation that is now collectively under the age of twenty-five.

Some would argue those born from, say, 1980 to the early 2000s are one giant cohort known as Millennials. It's true that such a grouping would be unified under a technology revolution, but as the research of Bruce Tulgan notes, "This time frame is simply too broad to define just one generation because the 1990s and the 2000s are two distinct eras."[5] To lump them together would be to link a thirteen-year-old with a thirty-five-year-old. And even technologically, that would be hard to embrace. Much of the 1990s was pre-internet (except for very, very early adopters). And the smartphone? Nonexistent. The ubiquitous nature of these two things alone would decisively divide any generation. "Growing up with a supercomputer in your pocket connected to most of the world's population and knowledge," writes David Pakman, "has created an irreversible pattern of behavior unlikely to revert to the ways of previous generations."[6] Or as an article in the *New York Times* noted, "A 14-year-old in 2015 really does inhabit a substantially different world than one of 2005."[7]

Intriguingly, some are calling Generation Z the last generation we will ever speak of. The speed of culture, in which change can happen in a day, will make speaking of generations and their markings obsolete. "Tomorrow will be less about what a difference a generation makes, but more about what a difference a day makes."[8] All the more reason to make sure we know about what is probably the last, and arguably what will prove to be the most influential, generation in Western history.

So who is Generation Z? They are growing up in a post-9/11 world. They are experiencing radical changes in technology and understandings of family, sexuality, and gender. They live in multigenerational households, and the fastest-growing demographic within their age group is multiracial. But let's unpack them a bit more slowly. Here are the five defining characteristics of Generation Z.

Defining Characteristics of Generation Z

Recession Marked

With most members of Generation Z born after 9/11, the most defining event in their lifetimes is the Great Recession. Beginning in 2007, this economic era is widely considered the worst global downturn since World War II. While Millennials were "raised during the boom times and relative peace of the 1990s, only to see their sunny world dashed by the September 11 attacks and two economic crashes, in 2000 and 2008 . . . Generation Z, by contrast," says the *New York Times*, "has had its eyes open from the beginning, coming along in the aftermath of those cataclysms in the era of the war on terror and the Great Recession."[9] This helps explain the (surprising to many) embrace of socialism among young voters in the 2016 presidential election, in marked contrast to older voters. A YouGov study found that 26 percent of those between the ages of eighteen and thirty-nine had a favorable view of socialism, compared to only 15 percent over the age of sixty-five.[10]

As members of Generation Z develop their personalities and life skills in a socioeconomic environment "marked by chaos, uncertainty, volatility, and complexity," it is no surprise that blockbusters like *The Hunger Games* and *Divergent*, with their depictions of teens left alone to face a dystopian future, connect with them. Simply put, they are deeply worried about the present.[11]

They are not alone.

The Public Religion Research Institute's annual American Values Survey "documents discontent among all major religious groups, races and political views." As PRRI CEO Robert Jones commented, "I am struck by the high level of anxiety and worry on all fronts." For the first time in six years of the survey, Americans are split—49 percent to 49 percent—on whether "America's best days are ahead of us or behind us. . . . Americans of all faiths and viewpoints are gloomy about the economy, anxious about Islam, bothered by immigrants and mistrustful across racial lines." And adding to the joy, more than seven out of ten (72 percent) believe that the country is still in a recession.[12] "No wonder," says the research report of Sparks and Honey, "Gen Z developed coping mechanisms and a certain resourcefulness."[13] Even when news broke of the widespread terrorist attacks in Paris in November 2015, the younger people I engaged were shocked but not surprised. There's a difference. And the difference is that attacks like these are not simply reality but what life has always been like.

Their coping mechanisms have led to a strong sense of independence and an entrepreneurial spirit. According to a study by Northeastern University, a "notable 42 percent of Generation Z respondents expect to work for themselves during their careers."[14] But their goal is not simply economic security. They are marked by a very strong sense of wanting to make a difference—and thinking that they can. Among the attendees at a recent Generation Z conference at American University in Washington, DC, was Sejal Makheja. At the age of fourteen, she founded the Elevator Project, an organization that aims to lift people out of poverty through apprenticeship, vocational training, and job placement. She said she went to the Gen Z conference because she wanted to cultivate the skills she'll need to take the Elevator Project to a national scale. "The young people at the conference want to take an active role in their communities and their futures," she said. "It's an upbeat group that's full of passion."[15] Not surprisingly, the research of Sparks and Honey reveals that social entrepreneurship is one of Generation Z's most popular career choices.[16]

This may explain why, when MTV conducted a nationwide survey of one thousand respondents born after the year 2000 to see how they would identify themselves if they had the choice, they came up with the self-important name "The Founders"—as in needing to "found the new world," rescuing it from the sins of its past.[17] For an immediate and inspiring introduction to this mindset, go no further than one of the many TED talks featuring teenagers sharing their visions and dreams for the future. For example, Logan LaPlante's presentation at TEDx at the University of Nevada on "Hackschooling" has been viewed on YouTube over nine million times as of the time of this writing. "Hackers are innovators," LaPlante said from the stage. "Hackers are people who challenge and change the system to make them work differently. To make them work better. . . . I'm growing up in a world that needs more people with a hacker mindset."[18]

Wi-Fi Enabled

It's no wonder that a term like *hacker* is being wielded in such broad ways. While it's still the early days for Generation Z, research from the Wharton School declares that "already one defining characteristic is abundantly clear: This generation is Wi-Fi enabled." Many refer to the Millennials as being "digital natives," due to their comfort and innate abilities with digital technology. But according to David Bell, professor of marketing at Wharton, Generation Z is the "Internet-in-its-pocket" generation.[19]

The speed by which this technological revolution has taken place is stunning and makes it difficult for older generations to realize the radically different world into which Generation Z has been born. As William Bernstein has pointed out, by 1960, only armies, governments, and very large organizations operated computers; by 1970, small organizations had acquired them. By 1980, hobbyists were happily assembling them from kits; by 1990, inexpensive personal computers had entered the home. By 2000, "most citizens of the developed world had access to the Internet."[20] Generation Z is the first generation that is the product of what Bernstein calls the fourth great communication revolution: the first was language itself, the second was writing, the third was the mechanization of writing, and the fourth was the electronic encoding of information.[21]

Currently, teenagers spend nearly nine hours a day absorbing media. And according to the teens themselves, Mom and Dad may care about the content of what they absorb but not the time spent on media itself.[22] In fact, parents seem to be the enablers. According to *eMarketer*, in the United States, kids are most likely to be gifted with gaming devices and TVs between ages four and seven. From the ages of eight to eleven, they will receive a gaming console, digital musical player, tablet, or e-reader. Twenty-two million twelve- to seventeen-year-olds in the United States alone owned a mobile device in 2015.[23]

While Baby Boomers can't remember a world without TV and Millennials can't remember a world without computers, "Gen Z does not know a world without constant, immediate and convenient access to the web."[24] When Steve Jobs announced the original iPhone as little more than a combination of "three revolutionary projects"—a cell phone, an iPod, and a keyboardless handheld computer with internet connectivity—even he didn't know what had been unleashed. Beyond the more than one million applications and counting,[25] it opened the door to what Brian Chen calls the

Figure 2.2

Craig Blankenhorn/HBO, via *Associated Press*   Eric McCandless/ABC

	Millennials (born 1980–95)	**Generation Z** (born 1996–2010)
TV ICON	Hannah Horvath, *Girls*	Alex Dunphy, *Modern Family*
MUSIC	Lady Gaga	Lorde
SOCIAL MEDIA	Facebook	Snapchat, Whisper
WEB STAR	PewDiePie, YouTube	Lele Pons, Vine
STYLE INFLUENCE	Olsen twins	Tavi Gevinson
CLOTHES	American Apparel	Shop Jeen
FIRST GADGET	iPod	iPhone

Source: Alex Williams, "Move Over Millennials: Here Comes Generation Z," *New York Times*, September 20, 2015, http://www.nytimes.com/2015/09/20/fashion/move-over-millennials-here-comes-generation-z.html.

"anything-anytime-anywhere future" in which we are constantly connected to a global internet community via handheld, incredibly capable gadgets with ubiquitous access to data. As he titles his book, we now live in a world that is "always on."[26]

This means a world with very few constraints, and members of Generation Z are taking advantage of it. Ninety-two percent report going online daily. A quarter say they go online "almost constantly."[27] Ninety-one percent go to bed with their devices.[28] No surprise that they also spend more money online than any other generation.[29] Yet the implications of this constant connection to the internet and, through it, the world and all of its information leads to another Generation Z dynamic: the "ability to find whatever they're after without the help of intermediaries—such as libraries, shops, or teachers." This has made them "more independent and self-directed than generations before them."[30]

Like no other generation before, Generation Z faces a widening chasm between wisdom and information. Quentin Schultze writes that the torrent of information now at our disposal is often little more than "endless volleys of nonsense, folly and rumor masquerading as knowledge, wisdom, and even truth."[31] Chuck Kelley, president of New Orleans Baptist Theological Seminary, has noted that "Google has changed the relationship of people to information. For the last three or four hundred years, information has been collected on college, university, and seminary campuses. . . . You went to the collected information to learn. Today the information is available anywhere you want, just Google it."[32] Kelley observes that the new task of education is to help students *evaluate* information. He's right. It is as if we've dropped a library card onto the world but removed the classroom that gives us the literacy to read its contents, much less the education needed to interpret its contents.

Then there is social media, which is not merely second nature to them; it is their primary nature. But unlike older participants in social media, they are not wed to any single social network. Further, they are much more private about things than their Millennial elders. They gravitate less toward Facebook than anonymous social media platforms such as Snapchat, Secret, and Whisper. As a *Mashable* article by Ruby Karp, a New York teenager, was titled, "I'm 13 and None of My Friends Use Facebook." According to a Pew study, a stunning 57 percent have never posted anything online due to privacy concerns.[33] Arguably, this is a result of seeing how permanent a footprint was left by older Millennials who often posted foolishly.

But because social media is their nature, so is seeking its immediate affirmation and acceptance, "since that's where all their peers are and where many of the important conversations happen," writes Jeremy Finch. "They curate different social media personas in order to please each audience and minimize conflict or controversy." Or as one sixteen-year-old from Arizona said, "We filter out whatever flaws we may have, to create the ideal image."[34]

According to Keith Niedermeier, adjunct professor of marketing at Wharton, Generation Z's time online, along with their extensive reliance on social media, means "they're also highly influenced by others' opinions and word of mouth."[35] In fact, while 29 percent still get most of their news from original online news sites like NYTimes.com or CNN.com, "a significant 27 percent receive their information primarily through word of mouth."[36] Sparks and Honey found that 52 percent of Generation Z even use social media for their research assignments in school.[37]

But don't think this means they are becoming distanced from personal interactions, much less relationships. Only 15 percent prefer to interact with their friends via social media rather than face-to-face. The vast majority also do not want to ask someone out on a date online or break off a relationship online.[38] While they relate to others through media, it is often through live streaming services such as FaceTime or Skype.

Multiracial

The United States is currently in the midst of a changing racial demographic, what some have called the fourth wave of immigration following the passage of immigration reform in 1965, which eliminated quotas based on nationality. The current wave is the largest in history, with the majority of these immigrants coming to our country from Mexico, Central America, and the Caribbean.[39] Between 2000 and 2010, the country's Hispanic population grew at four times the rate of the total population. In 2006, there was a record number of births in the United States, and 49 percent of those born were Hispanic. Since the early 1700s, the most common last name in the United States was Smith, but now it is Rodriguez.[40]

But this trend is about more than immigration. The number of Americans self-identifying as white and black multiracial rose 134 percent. The number of Americans of mixed white and Asian descent grew by 87 percent.[41] There has been a 400 percent increase in black-white multiracial marriages in the last thirty years and a 1,000 percent increase in Asian-white marriages. Overall, multiracial children are the fastest-growing youth group in the United States.[42] When the 2020 census is conducted, it is estimated that more than half of all US children will be part of a minority race or ethnic group.[43]

As a result, Generation Z is the most racially diverse of any generation to date. As a writer for the Bloomberg News put it, "It may be the first generation for which diversity is a natural concept."[44] They are globally connected, which means their social circles are often global. Or as one research project put it, "26 percent of Gen Z would need to fly to visit most of their social network friends."[45] This diversity also leads to being "accepting" and "inclusive." Some have described this as the "Kumbaya" dynamic, members of Generation Z standing in a circle holding hands. They are connected to people around them and aware of the world beyond themselves.[46]

Sexually Fluid

The accepting nature of Generation Z leads to strong support for such things as gay marriage and transgender rights. They are coming of age in the era that has put such things in the mainstream, such as in 2015 when the Supreme Court legalized gay marriage and former-Olympian-turned-reality-TV-star Bruce Jenner very publicly became Caitlyn Jenner. Indeed, according to the Northeastern University study, the "question of same-sex marriage is decisively settled for them, with 73 percent in favor. Notably, they also support equal rights for transgender people in high numbers (74 percent)."[47] For Generation Z, the idea of "acceptance" is often interchangeable with the idea of "affirmation."

Yet it would be a mistake to see Generation Z as simply the product of an abrupt social change related to such headlines. As Michael

Gerson and Peter Wehner have noted, when the Supreme Court decided in *Obergefell v. Hodges* that the Constitution guarantees a right to same-sex marriage, it was the result of cultural trends that emerged in the context of heterosexual, not homosexual, relationships. "Marriage was not redefined only by the Supreme Court," they write. "It was also redefined by decades of social practice." In other words, decades of radical individualism—particularly in sexual ethics—that resulted in a "shift in attitudes, behavior, and laws on divorce, abortion, cohabitation, out-of-wedlock births, gender roles, and now, decisively, same-sex marriage."[48] Translation: Generation Z is the cultural product of decisions made by earlier generations as opposed to their own.

Nonetheless, from this shift in attitudes and behaviors Generation Z has become sexually and relationally amorphous. Consider the influential statements by outspoken young celebrities such as Kristen Stewart, Miley Cyrus, and Cara Delevingne. Stewart, when asked about her sexuality, said, "I think in three or four years, there are going to be a whole lot more people who don't think it's necessary to figure out if you're gay or straight. It's like, just do your thing." And from Miley Cyrus: I don't "relate to being boy or girl, and I don't have to have my partner relate to boy or girl."[49]

They are not alone.

A recent UK study revealed that nearly half of all young people don't think they are exclusively heterosexual. The YouGov survey revealed that 49 percent of people between the ages of eighteen and twenty-four identified as something other than 100 percent heterosexual. This despite the repeated findings that only about 4 percent of the entire adult population is actually homosexual. What is being revealed is an increasing sexual fluidity that refuses either the homosexual or the heterosexual label. The idea is that both labels are repressive. Sexuality should be set free from any and all restrictions, and people should be allowed to follow their desires, moment by moment.[50]

Why? Because the greatest value for this generation is nothing less than individual freedom. So don't be misled by the studies reporting that they don't drink, smoke, take drugs, or sleep around (and to be sure, their percentages on each are lower than previous generations). They are not, in any way, socially conservative philosophically.

Beyond what we've already detailed, it is interesting how marketing firms package their conclusions regarding Generation Z. For example, according to the marketing research of Sparks and Honey, here are the top "Z" headlines:[51]

- They are eager to start working.
- They are mature and in control.
- They intend to change the world.
- They've learned that traditional choices don't guarantee success.
- Entrepreneurship is in their DNA.
- They seek education and knowledge, and they use social media as a research tool.
- They multitask across five screens, and their attention spans are getting shorter.
- They think spatially and in 4D but lack situational awareness.
- They communicate with symbols, speed, and images.
- Their social circles are global.
- They are hyperaware and concerned about humanity's impact on the planet.
- They are less active and frequently obese.
- They live stream and cocreate.

All true, but this is a very tame list—quite frankly, one you would expect from a marketing firm. And not surprisingly, it misses the biggest headline of all, which constitutes the fifth and final defining mark of Generation Z.

Post-Christian

The most defining characteristic of Generation Z is that it is arguably the first generation in the West (certainly in the United States) that will have been raised in a post-Christian context. As a result, it is the first post-Christian generation.

Yes, most people of Generation Z still believe in the existence of God (78 percent). But less than half attend weekly religious services of any kind (41 percent), and only 8 percent would cite a religious leader as a role model.[52] The largest single religious category in the *Harvard Crimson*'s "by the numbers" survey of the class of 2019 was "agnostic" (21.3 percent).[53] Recall the statistics from the previous chapter: the younger the demographic, the greater the percentage who fall into the category of the religiously unaffiliated—the nones. And, Pew reports, they do not seem to be growing more religiously observant as they get older.[54] As the research of the Barna Group concluded, the "pattern is indisputable: The younger the generation, the more post-Christian it is."[55]

Discussion Questions

1. Did the findings from the Beloit College freshmen survey surprise you? Were you aware of the vast differences between this generation and your own?
2. Generation Z is the largest generation alive today. Those in this generation will not simply influence American culture; they will constitute American culture. How does that reality impact the way you view Generation Z?
3. What is the defining event for those in Generation Z? How does that affect their worldview?
4. At the time of this writing, teenagers are spending nearly nine hours a day absorbing media. What implications does

this have for reaching them for Christ and bringing them into the church?

5. Have you ever reflected on how constant, easy, and immediate access to the internet through smartphones and other devices is shaping younger generations? How should this change the church's approach to equipping parents?

6. What was the most surprising finding about Generation Z to you? Why? And what does it mean for your ministry?

7. What is the greatest value for Generation Z? How does this value prevent obstacles to the gospel? How does it present opportunities?

3

When Christ
and His Saints Slept

Never before had there been greater wretchedness in the country.
. . . And they said openly that Christ and his saints slept.

Peterborough Chronicle (twelfth century)

There is a dynamic to understanding Generation Z and its members' spiritual condition that is almost entirely overlooked by those seeking to study their character and disposition.

This dynamic is the manner in which they are being raised.

One of the marks of Generation Z is that they are being raised, by and large, by Generation X—a generation that was warned repeatedly not to become "helicopter" parents (i.e., always hovering over their children). As a result, Generation Z has been given more space and more independence than any other generation. This means that Generation Z is very self-directed.[1]

Consider the free-range parenting movement, a hands-off approach to parenting that entered the cultural mainstream largely through an article by a *New York Sun* columnist who let her nine-year-old son ride the New York subway alone. She handed him "a subway map, a Metrocard, a $20 bill, and several quarters, just in case he had to make a call." She purposefully skipped the cell phone and didn't trail him like a "mommy private eye." She then celebrated his safe return, ecstatic with his independence.[2] The response to her article led to the creation of the FreeRangeKids .com website, which led to free-range approaches to every aspect of parenting, including letting children take the lead in what they learn, what they eat, and what media they consume.

Perhaps particularly what media they consume.

As one father described his parenting world, after ensuring that his six-year-old daughter was on the family iPad, his eight- and eleven-year-old sons were on the PlayStation, and his two-year-old was watching something on his iPhone, "For me, this was a good morning's parenting. There had been no arguments and I had been able to read the papers in peace." To his thinking, any other way of parenting "just isn't realistic." Why? The "world has moved on." Since it's not always safe to let children venture outside, where they might run or play or use their imagination, children simply have to "spend more time in front of a screen."

Granted, the author continues, they could go outside or engage in reading, but such an endeavor "invariably involves parental supervision, and that is a limited resource." So technology comes to the rescue, offering parents a way to occupy their children that does not involve direct parental supervision.[3] As one pediatrician remarked about the time children spend on screens, "It [is] time to stop arguing over whether it was good or bad and accept it as part of children's environment."[4]

The Underprotective Parent

If Millennials were raised by overprotective parents, then Generation Z is being raised by underprotective parents. It's as if the one thing you don't want to do as a parent is to be (using the pejorative words of the day) hovering, smothering, babying, coddling, or sheltering. The insinuation is that it's wrong to be overprotective, but it's not wrong to be underprotective. If you're going to make a mistake, make a mistake in being loose, in playing fast and free, and in not protecting enough. Because the one big parenting sin is believed to be protecting too much.

Reflect on this in relation to Generation Z. In other words, consider the effect of an underprotective family environment in a day of sexting and Facebook, bullying in schools and internet porn, cutting and hooking up. When children need to be protected as never before, they are met with a parenting culture that is less protective than at any other time in recent history.

The proper assumption with regard to parenting is simple: children are immature and need parental maturity. Parents are to be informed, involved, and in charge. Children are not little adults; they are children. Consider how the following list of rules parents should follow regarding kids and technology would be perceived by the average parent today:

1. Limit their phone minutes, texts, and online hours. Don't let their phones take over their lives.
2. Don't ever let them see a movie you haven't reviewed thoroughly on the front end, regardless of its rating.
3. Don't let them sleep with their cell phones under their pillows or by their beds. Phones should be turned off at bedtime.
4. Have times of the day when they have to turn their phones off and times when texting isn't allowed—such as family vacations or family outings.
5. Don't allow cell phones at the dinner table.
6. Tell your kids not to share their passwords with their friends, not even their best friends.
7. Keep all computer use in a public area.

8. Don't allow TVs in their rooms.

9. Don't let them be on Facebook unless they friend you.

10. Don't let them join any social media prior to the stated age.

Even half of these rules would be considered almost unthinkable to the average parent of a Generation Z child, which means that in the name of freedom and independence, Generation Z is growing up with the entirety of the world in their vision. As a result, childhood slowly evaporates. Or as Neil Postman writes, in having access to the previously hidden fruit of adult information, the child is expelled from the garden of childhood.[5]

But the self-directed nature of Generation Z isn't simply a by-product of the change in parenting from "helicopter" to "free range." It's about the changing nature of childhood itself.

The Disappearance of Childhood

I once recall reading two articles in the span of twenty-four hours that charted different, seemingly benign ways that the nature of childhood is changing. The first was titled "Children Losing a Love of Stories in the Digital Age," and the second was "Game Is Up for Traditional Pastimes with Half-Hour Version of Monopoly."[6] In the first article, in regard to the digital age, educators lamented how children "exposed to iPads, 3D films, and game consoles are losing interest in traditional storytelling." They cannot read in silence or listen to stories because they are growing up in a world containing "endless distraction." Yet it is a love of reading that increases concentration and promotes "deep thinking."

The second article charted how the toy company Hasbro, in a day of smartphone apps, social media, and short attention spans, determined that children cannot handle long games. So the latest version of Monopoly was tweaked to find a winner in thirty minutes. A commentary at Gizmodo.com lamented the passing of one of the "cornerstones of childhood." If only that were true. In reality, these are just pale reflections of the real loss of childhood taking place in our world.

One of Neil Postman's most provocative works was titled *The Disappearance of Childhood*. His thesis was that children are being robbed of their innocence, their naïveté, their ability even to *be* a child. He contended that in our world, we ask children to embrace mature issues, themes, and experiences long before they are ready.

Postman argued that the very idea of childhood is that there is a time when young people are sheltered from certain ideas, experiences, practices, expectations, and knowledge. They are sheltered from adult secrets, particularly sexual ones. Certain facets of life—its mysteries, contradictions, tragedies, violence—are not considered suitable for children to know. Only as children grow into adulthood are such facets revealed in ways that children can assimilate psychologically, emotionally, and spiritually.

Postman's analysis, first offered in 1982, was prescient. Today twelve- and thirteen-year-old girls are among the highest paid models in America, presented to us as knowing and sexually enticing adults. Much young adult fiction is as mature in its themes as anything on the adult lists. The language of adults and children—including what they address in life—has become the same. It is virtually uncontested among sociologists that the behavior, language, attitudes, and desires—even the physical appearance—of adults and children are becoming indistinguishable. Even the children on TV act like adults. They do not differ significantly in their interests, language, dress, or sexuality from the adults on the show, making the same knowing wisecracks and tossing out the same sexual innuendo.

This is why for years the books that were read in the fourth grade or seventh grade or ninth grade were chosen not only for their vocabulary and syntax but also because their content was considered to contain fourth-, seventh-, or ninth-grade information, ideas, and experiences. But when the line between the adult world and the world of children becomes blurred or no longer exists, childhood disappears.

Growing Older Younger

What has been the result of the disappearance of childhood?[7] This can be summed up with a simple acronym: G.O.Y. (Grow Older Younger). Sometimes referred to as K.G.O.Y. (Kids Getting Older Younger), it is something that we see played out more and more in the culture of the day. As Pamela Paul wrote in the *New York Times*, "G.O.Y. [has six-year-olds going to school guidance counselors] complaining that So-and-So won't play with them because they like the Jonas Brothers and the 'It girls' like Miley Cyrus."[8] So culture is now dictating that at six, it is more age appropriate to keep up with Lady Gaga than *Lady and the Tramp*.

Tracy Vaillancourt, who specializes in children's mental health at the University of Ottawa, says, "Kids mirror the larger culture, from reality TV to materialism."[9] Who they see is who they want to be.

And the influence of their peers can be utterly overwhelming. As their closest friends succumb to the trend of G.O.Y., many children feel pressured to match them for the sake of popularity and acceptance. And sadly, instead of stepping in to be the voice of reason, many parents are feeding into this cultural trend.

Many parents, wishing their children to *fit* in, begin to *give* in, thus escalating the downward spiral, because the truth is that parents can be just as quick to give in to the trap of peer pressure as their children:

- Parents don't want their child to have a smartphone yet, but every other kid has one.

- Parents don't want their child to see *that* movie, but everyone else in their class will be seeing it over the weekend and talking about it on Monday morning.
- Parents aren't crazy about the latest fashion trend, but they don't want their child to be singled out.

While parents know what they should do, want to do, and feel is best to do for their child, around every corner they are confronted by what everyone else is doing. The choice becomes to either swim upstream or go with the current.

The Soundtrack to Their Lives

It is helpful to remember the way such exposure, especially exposure to media, actually works. The great communications theorist Marshall McLuhan wrote, "All media work us over completely." He added, "They are so pervasive in their personal, political, economic, aesthetic, psychological, moral, ethical, and social consequences that they leave no part of us untouched, unaffected, unaltered."[10] Fred Fedler, author of one of the most widely used college textbooks on mass media, says that "the media may constitute the most powerful education system ever known to man."[11] Or as MTV founder Bob Pittman once said, "At MTV, we don't shoot for the 14-year-olds, we own them."[12]

So how is that media shaping this new generation?

It's difficult to know for sure at this point, but at the very least, we know what it is attempting to convey. Take a moment to Google the lyrics for the top iTunes downloads. I think you will be shocked at what you find. Between the sexually explicit lyrics and the use of expletives, they are far from innocuous.

But without a doubt, the most pervasive and influential aspect of media shaping Generation Z in a way no other generation has been shaped is pornography, and this is where underprotective parenting may be leaving its most lasting mark.

Pornography

Being the first generation with a connection to the internet in their pockets has, as you would imagine, its dark side—namely, the ubiquitous presence and availability of pornography. No other generation has had pornography so available, in such extremes, at such a young age. Seventy percent of all eighteen- to thirty-four-year-olds are regular viewers. The average age to begin viewing? Eleven.[13] It's been called the "wallpaper of our lives." In 2014, one porn site alone had over 15.35 billion visits. No, that was not a typo. That's "billion" with a *b*.[14] To put that into perspective, at the end of 2015, the entire population of the world was just over seven billion.

The degree to which members of Generation Z live in a pornified world and are themselves immersed in it as a "new normal" was revealed in the 2015 Cybercrime Tipping Point report, which found that sixteen- to seventeen-year-olds were not overly concerned about revenge porn (when explicit photos from a previous relationship are posted online without consent). For them, the larger issues were hacking or fraud. The report concluded that revenge porn was nothing more than an "everyday concern" for modern teens.[15] But even though Generation Z may not be worried about porn, those who care about the generation should be.

Research has clearly established that teens who watch movies or listen to music that glamorizes drinking, drug use, or violence tend to engage in those behaviors themselves. A 2012 study showed that movies also influence teens' sexual attitudes and behaviors. A study published in *Psychological Science* found that the more teens were exposed to sexual content in movies, the earlier they started having sex and the likelier they were to have casual, unprotected sex.[16]

In terms of pornography, boys who were exposed to sexually explicit media were three times more likely to engage in oral sex and intercourse two years after exposure than nonexposed boys. Young girls exposed to sexual content in the media were twice as likely to engage in oral sex and one and a half times more likely to have intercourse. Research also has shown that teens who listened to music with degrading sexual references were more likely to have sex than those who had less exposure. Beyond sexual activity, similar research has found that early viewing of pornography among children leads to higher-risk sexual activity, sex addictions, and sexual violence.[17]

So what else is pornography doing to them? We don't fully know as yet. As Eric Schmidt and Jared Cohen opened their book *The New Digital Age*, "The Internet is among the few things humans have built that they don't truly understand. . . . [It is] the largest experiment involving anarchy in history."[18] But what we do know is deeply disturbing. Chloe Combi, a former school teacher and consultant on youth issues for the mayor of London, interviewed hundreds from Generation Z. Her blunt conclusion: "They're almost certainly imitating what they see in pornography."[19] For example, according to research from La Trobe University's Research Centre in Sex, Health, and Society (tasked by the Australian government), nearly three-quarters of fifteen- to eighteen-year-olds have sexted, and half have sent naked or seminaked photos and videos of themselves. Eighty-four percent have received sexually explicit messages by phone or email. The report also found that 70 percent of the surveyed teenagers were sexually active and that nearly three-quarters of those did not regret having sex. Anne Mitchell, author of the report, said, "It's a social, online world kids live in and sending these images and messages is part of the sexual relationship so it's really a new form of courtship."[20]

In her book *Pornified*, Pamela Paul agrees, arguing that pornography has changed our marriages and families as well as our children's understanding of sex and sexuality. Her portraits are riveting:

> Rob, who insists that his girlfriend look and behave, in bed and out, like a porn star; Charlie, who spends hours cruising porn sites and setting up meetings with women and couples he befriends in chat rooms, while telling his wife that he's just working late on the computer; Jonah, a fan of violent hardcore porn, who introduces tamer porn to his fiancée in an effort to revive their troubled sex life; Abby, who discovers her husband's hidden box of CD's of child porn images downloaded from the internet; preteen girls who start their own pornography websites; teenage boys, mimicking porn, who videotape themselves having sex with an apparently unconscious girl.[21]

Let's state the obvious: this is sexual sin. Jesus made it clear that when we give in to lust, it is akin to the act of sex itself. It makes no difference whether we know the person or not; lust is not tied to relationship. So pornography may be the greatest area of immorality inflicted on and pursued by Generation Z.

And the cause for concern is great because we know that porn is highly addictive.[22] In fact, 94 percent of all therapists are reporting dramatic increases in the number of people addicted to online pornography.[23] The ease of access to porn is greater than ever before, and for Generation Z that comes in the form of a smart phone sitting in their pocket at all times. Porn is something that can dominate the thought lives of those in its grasp, leading them to need ever-increasing degrees of exposure and experience to provide the same level of stimulation over time.

Porn is not only addictive but also incredibly degrading to women and sends a message to younger children—boys and girls alike—that women are nothing more than mere objects. Susan Fiske, professor of psychology at Princeton University, used MRI scans to analyze men watching pornography. Afterward, brain activity revealed they looked at women more as objects than as people.[24] What is entirely overlooked is that these women (and men as well) are being treated in a way that is contemptible to their heavenly Father and breaks his heart.

Southern Baptist pastor Denny Burk, as quoted in an article in the *American Conservative*, said, "A growing number of young men are convinced that their sexual responses have been sabotaged because their brains were virtually marinated in porn when they were adolescents. Their generation has consumed explicit content in quantities and varieties never before possible, on devices designed to deliver content swiftly and privately, all at an age when their brains were more plastic—more prone to permanent change—than in later life."[25] This has led to men becoming sexually more aggressive, leading to date rapes and expected hookups. In other words, what we *view* can quickly become what we *do*.

Finally, what may be one of the most troubling effects of pornography is that it desensitizes your soul. And while it is true that sin of any kind desensitizes your spiritual life, the Bible discusses how particularly harmful sexual sin is. The apostle Paul writes, "There is a sense in which sexual sins are different from all others. In sexual sins we violate the sacredness of our own bodies, these bodies that were made for God-given and God-modeled love, for 'becoming one' with another. Or didn't you realize that your body is a sacred place, the place of the Holy Spirit?" (1 Cor. 6:18–19 Message). So those who are a part of Generation Z are post-Christian not only in both spirit and context, they are also uniquely immersed in and embracing a form of sin that is poised to deaden them spiritually.

But that's not all.

The None Parent

As detailed in the opening chapter, a large and growing number of parents—particularly parents of Generation Z—are themselves in the nones category. So how does an underprotective parent who is religiously unaffiliated raise a child spiritually? Not well. As journalist Ruth Graham started her article for *Slate*, "I'm the kind of Christian that many adults warned me about as a child: I've been a church member for most of my adult life, but I have at times gone years without regular attendance, my theology is squishy, and I don't really pray, to name just a few qualities that put me on the breezy outer edge of Christianity's big tent. I think of myself as 'religious but not spiritual.'"[26]

This, as we explored in the opening chapter, is a textbook description of the spirituality of a typical none. And as I detailed in my book *The Rise of the Nones*, the real mark of the nones is not a rejection of God but a rejection of any specific religion. When it comes to content, dogma, orthodoxy—anything spelled out or offering a system of beliefs—they've gone from "I believe" to "Maybe" to "Who knows?" When pressed as to what they do hold to, they collectively answer, "Nothing in particular."

Simply put, they are spiritual but not religious.

They may not want to say, "I'm a Baptist," but that does not equate with, "I don't believe in God." In other words, there is a strong reticence toward labels of any kind. It might help to visualize this in terms of a religious axis and a spiritual axis, creating four quadrants (see fig. 3.1).

The caricature of the nones would place them in the "not religious, not spiritual" category, but that would be inaccurate. The vast majority belong in the "not religious, spiritual" quadrant.

"Not religious, spiritual" is not a disavowal of faith or belief. Instead, it is the rejection of a label related to faith or belief. In years past, an unchurched individual might still claim to be Baptist or Catholic. Now there is great cultural freedom to drop the label entirely. The speed with which this has happened supports an old thesis of church historian Martin Marty, who wrote a book half a century ago on varieties of unbelief and who thought that religious cohesion "has long been overstated."[27]

Figure 3.1

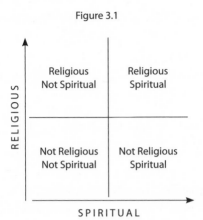

John Green, a senior research adviser at Pew, breaks the religiously unaffiliated into three groups: First are those who were raised totally outside organized religion. Second are those who became unhappy with their religions and left. And lastly are those who never really engaged with religion in the first place, even though they were raised in religious households. "In the past, we would describe those people as nominally affiliated. They might say, 'I am Catholic; I am a Baptist,' but they never went [to services]. Now, they feel a lot more comfortable just saying, 'You know, I am really nothing.'"[28]

So what of Generation Z? Or more particularly, their parents? As Ruth Graham went on to write, "Somehow the gruel-thin texture of my adult faith has never troubled me. Or at least not until this summer, when my infant daughter careened into my life—including my spiritual life, such as it is." She reflected that she wanted her child to know certain religious stories and songs, almost out of nostalgia for her own childhood, but "I don't want her to be afraid of a hell I don't believe in, and I don't want to lie about what I believe." She ended by saying, "I dread the day when my daughter asks me if the stories in the Bible are true. My real answer is that some of them are and some of them sort of are and some of them aren't. . . . That should work for a 3-year-old, right?"[29]

No, it shouldn't.

But it's what we have to work with.

When Christ and His Saints Slept

During the calamitous twelfth century, it was written that "there was never more wretched [people] on this land." The writer then added, "And they said openly that Christ and his saints slept."[30]

One might be tempted to say the same of our own day, particularly in relation to how we are shaping Generation Z. There are many ways to characterize them, but in essence, two headlines must not be missed. First, they are lost. They are not simply living in and being shaped by a post-Christian cultural context. They do not even have a memory of the gospel. The degree of spiritual illiteracy is simply stunning. Stephen Prothero, chairman of the religion department of Boston University, once wrote of regularly administering a fifteen-question quiz to his undergraduate students. The quiz included the following:[31]

Name the four Gospels.

Where according to the Bible was Jesus born?

President George W. Bush spoke in his first inaugural address of the Jericho road. What Bible story was he invoking?

What are the first five books of the Hebrew Bible or the Christian Old Testament?

What is the Golden Rule?

"God helps those who help themselves." Is this in the Bible? If so, where?

"Blessed are the poor in spirit, for theirs is the kingdom of God." Does this appear in the Bible?

Name the Ten Commandments.

Needless to say, most of his students didn't have a clue. Today I doubt first-year seminary students would have a clue. Imagine how Generation Z would fare?

But second, they are leaderless. Little if any direction is coming from their families, and even less from their attempts to access guidance from the internet. The questions I hear from men and women in their teens and twenties border on the heartbreaking. How do I break free from pornography? How do I be a husband/wife? How do I parent? How do I pray? How do I . . .? The list of life's most foundational questions is virtually endless, and Generation Z is asking each and every one. They have endless amounts of information but little wisdom, and virtually no mentors.

So how can they be reached?

It is to that task we now turn.

Discussion Questions

1. You read that Generation Z is growing up being very self-directed as a result of several cultural trends. Do you find that to be the case when thinking about young people you know?

2. Do you see evidence around you of childhood disappearing? What does that look like? How can your church partner with parents to face cultural pressures that lead to that disappearance?

3. Did you take some time to look up the lyrics for the most popular downloads on iTunes? If so, what was your reaction when you read them? What are some practical ways you can stay current with things such as music, movies, and TV (not necessarily *experiencing* them but being *aware* of them)?

4. The numbers surrounding pornography are staggering: 70 percent of all eighteen- to thirty-four-year-olds are regular

viewers; the average age to begin viewing it is eleven. What implications does this have for those in any generation? How can you make sure you are addressing pornography in your ministry, whether through sermon illustrations, recovery ministries, or something else?

5. What does it mean that nones are in the category of "not religious, spiritual"? What implications does that have for their understandings of Christianity and the church?

6. Those in Generation Z do not even have a memory of the gospel. Let that sink in. How does that make you feel? Why might that be an opportunity and not just a frightening reality?

7. What about Generation Z leaves you hopeful for the future of the church?

PART 2

A NEW APPROACH

4

The Countercultural Church

I will put together my church, a church so expansive with energy
that not even the gates of hell will be able to keep it out.

Jesus (Matt. 16:18 Message)

In writing about the teaching of Jesus, John Stott noted that "if
the church realistically accepted his standards and values . . . and
lived by them, it would be the alternative society he always intended it to be, and would offer to the world an authentic Christian counter-culture."[1]

Those two ideas—church and counterculture—lie at the heart
of reaching a post-Christian generation. The challenge is, first, to
understand the ideas and, second, to engage them. Let's start with
understanding, for if there is any doctrine that is ignored or grossly
misunderstood by Christ followers—at least among evangelical
Christians in the United States—it is the doctrine of the church.

I remember, when I was a seminary president, sitting in a board-
room with a prominent Christian business leader and trying to

pitch a vision for him to contribute to theological education, specifically student scholarships.[2] Instead of listening to the opportunity or asking pertinent questions as to the value of such an investment, he was determined to boast of his company's identity as a Christian enterprise. He told of the mission trips he had taken with his employees, the investments his company had made in select boutique parachurch ventures, and the Bible study offered on campus for employees. Throughout his self-congratulatory spiel, he took more than his fair share of shots at local churches and pastors who were not as "alive" as he and members of his company were in their faith.

At the time, as a new seminary president facing an inherited budgetary shortfall of over one million dollars, I was willing to endure almost anything—or anyone—for aid. Then in the midst of one of his personal asides about the sorry state of the church, as compared to the pristine missional nature of his business, he maintained that it was for this reason that he wasn't involved in a local church. They were, he intimated, beneath his own theological vision. "And after all," he added, "we're the church too."

And then everything within me wanted to leap from my seat, shout, "Enough!," and say, "No, you are not!" As I wrote in *Christ Among the Dragons*:

> A company is *not* the body of Christ instituted as the hope of the world by Jesus Himself, chronicled breathtakingly by Luke through the book of Acts, and shaped in thinking and practice by the apostle Paul through letter after letter now captured in the New Testament. A marketplace venture which offers itself on the New York Stock Exchange is not the entity which is so expansive with energy that not even the gates of hell can withstand its onslaught. An assembly of employees in cubicles working for end-of-year stock options and bonuses is not the gathering of saints bristling with the power of spiritual gifts as they mobilize to provide justice for the oppressed, service to the widow and the orphan, and compassion for the poor.

I then added these words:

With jaw-dropping vigor, ignorance, and at times unblushing gall,
increasing sectors of the evangelical world are abandoning two
thousand years of ecclesiology as if the church was some malleable human construct that can be shaped, altered, redefined or
even disposed of as desired. This, coupled with a radical revision-
ism in terms of biblical interpretation and ecclesial history that
would seem more in line with *The Da Vinci Code* than Christian
theology, the doctrine of the church is being reformulated apart
from biblical moorings, or simply dismissed as if not a part of
biblical orthodoxy at all.

I stand by those words.

The Idea of Church

The word *church*, from the Greek word *ecclesia*, literally means
"the called-out ones."[3] It is a word that was used in Jesus's day
for any group that was gathered together for a specific purpose
or mission. Jesus seized the term to speak of a group with a *very*
specific purpose or mission, setting it apart from every other group
or mission. This is where *ecclesiology*, which is the theological
term for the doctrine of the church, finds its origin. The church of
Christ is anything but a man-made organization; it was founded
and instituted by Jesus himself (Matt. 16:18).

In the Bible, there are three primary understandings of this
church: the local church; the universal church as it exists around
the world; and the church as it exists throughout time and history,
incorporating all the saints who will one day be gathered together
in heaven. Without question, the dominant biblical use is in reference to a local church, or collection of local churches, as a defined
body of believers who are gathered with both intent and order.
Think of how the letters of Paul were written: "to the church of

God at Corinth," "to the churches in Galatia," "to the church of the Thessalonians." And John's Revelation begins, "To the seven churches in the province of Asia."

This church is to serve as the ongoing manifestation of Christ himself on earth, being called his body, an idea of profound significance throughout the New Testament. As the apostle Paul writes, "Just as each of us has one body with many members, and these members do not all have the same function, so in Christ we, though many, form one body, and each member belongs to all the others. We have different gifts, according to the grace given to each of us" (Rom. 12:4–6). Later in the New Testament, Paul reiterates this idea: "Now you are the body of Christ, and each one of you is a part of it" (1 Cor. 12:27). And if the point hadn't been made clearly enough, Paul writes the following words to the church at Ephesus: "And God placed all things under his feet and appointed him to be head over everything for the church, which is his body, the fullness of him who fills everything in every way" (Eph. 1:22–23; see also 5:23; Col. 1:18; 2:19).

Beyond the interconnectedness these passages suggest, they convey that the church is the locus of Christ's activity, and he works through the church now as he worked through his physical body during his thirty-three-year life. In the New Testament, there is simply no ministry outside the church, or at least its umbrella.

But what is this "local" church that functions as the body of Christ?

The earliest church, in the first forty or so years following the resurrection of Jesus, was essentially a movement within Judaism that believed the Messiah had come. But then, around AD 70, Jerusalem fell to the Romans, and the Christian church was dispersed. The most important church that emerged, as you would imagine, was the one in Rome, which was the capital of the Roman Empire.

During the next few centuries, the church defined itself by four very important words: *one*, *holy*, *catholic*, and *apostolic*. Each word carries great significance.[4] First, the church was to be one, or unified. Jesus, in his great and grand final prayer recorded in John's Gospel, prayed fervently for unity among those of us who would embrace his name in years and centuries to come. Second, it was to be a holy church, meaning set apart for God and separate from the world, for God himself is holy. The church was to reflect this holiness to the degree that it could be identified with God as holy. Third, the church was to be catholic, which simply means "universal." The church was meant to be a worldwide church, one that included all believers under its umbrella. So the word *catholic* was being used of the church long before any kind of institution within Christianity used it for its own. Finally, the church was to be apostolic, which means committed to the teaching handed down by Jesus through the apostles.

Beyond being one, holy, catholic, and apostolic, local churches were entities that had definition and form, structure and purpose. They were not simply doing "community" in the broadest of senses, much less simply pursuing ministry. In the Bible, the church was a defined, purposeful gathering of believers who knew they were coming together to *be* a church. There were defined entry and exit points to the church; clear theological guidelines navigating corporate and community waters; the responsibility of stewarding the sacraments; specifically named leadership positions; and, of course, a singular mission.

A very singular mission.

The church's mission, given by Jesus himself, is to reach out to a deeply fallen world and call it back to God. According to the Bible, this involves active evangelism with subsequent discipleship, coupled with strategic service to those in need, such as the poor. We are to be the body of Christ to this world, and the twin dynamics of evangelism and social concern reflect Christ's ongoing mission. And it is this cause that may be the most defining mark of all. Theologian Jürgen Moltmann reminds us that the church does not "have" a mission; rather, the mission "has" us.[5] And it is the mission of Christ that creates the church. God sent himself and now sends us. This is the *missio Dei*, the "sending of God." Or as Christopher J. H. Wright contends, our mission "means our committed participation as God's people, at God's invitation and command, in God's own mission within the history of God's world for the redemption of God's creation."[6] So to engage the mission of God is to engage his church; they are inextricably intertwined.

Which is why no conversation about reaching anyone, much less Generation Z, can proceed apart from the church. And there is no need to be awkward about being the church. The massive Pew study on the American religious landscape found that "most Americans continue to view organized religion as a force for good in American society." As the table below indicates, nearly nine out of ten adults said that "churches and other religious institutions bring people together and strengthen community bonds and that they play an important role in helping the poor and needy." A surprising three-quarters added that "churches and other religious institutions help protect and strengthen morality in society." These numbers were surprisingly robust and positive even among the religiously unaffiliated. So approaching Generation Z as the church and in the name of the church is not in and of itself a barrier. Indeed, it is their only hope, for it will take the body of Christ in its fullness to reach them.

Nonetheless, there are barriers to overcome. Specifically, the accompanying perception that churches are "too concerned with money and power, too involved in politics and too focused on rules."[7] But the most pressing barriers to overcome are more foundational—namely, the barriers that come from being compromised, cloistered, or combative. As for being compromised, the church will have to understand that the key is being "counter" to a post-Christian culture, not a copy of it, or else we will have nothing to offer the world that it does not already have. In terms of

Religious Institutions Widely Viewed
as Forces for Societal Good

Percent who agree that churches and other religious institutions . . .

	Bring people together and strengthen community bonds	Play important role in helping poor and needy	Protect and strengthen morality in society
Total	89	87	75
Christian Faiths	92	90	83
Protestant	93	91	85
Evangelical	94	92	87
Mainline	93	91	82
Historically black	89	88	81
Catholic	91	89	82
Orthodox Christian	93	87	74
Mormon	97	94	92
Jehovah's Witness	57	68	41
Non-Christian Faiths	86	82	62
Jewish	88	85	63
Muslim	88	89	83
Buddhist	86	78	65
Hindu	88	81	73
Unaffiliated	81	78	54
Atheist	75	71	31
Agnostic	85	84	52
Nothing in particular*	81	78	59
Religion not important	78	76	50
Religion important	86	81	71

*Those who describe their religion as "nothing in particular" are subdivided into two groups. The "religion not important" group includes those who say (in Q F2) religion is "not too" or "not at all" important in their lives as well as those who decline to answer the question about religion's importance. The "religion important" category includes those who say religion is "very" or "somewhat" important in their lives.

Source: 2014 Religious Landscape Study, conducted June 4–September 30, 2014, Pew Research Center. These questions were not asked in the 2007 Landscape Study.

being cloistered, we must avoid abdicating from cultural engagement by going into isolation. When it comes to being combative, we must avoid engaging culture in some kind of holy war. To be truly countercultural, in a manner impactful on a post-Christian generation, the church will need to take an approach that is entirely different from the three just described.

I will explore compromise in the next chapter, but for now, let's ensure we know what it means to be culturally engaged instead of cloistered or combative. These are such ongoing temptations that the church's recent history with such cultural ploys is worth recalling.

Remembering Fundamentalism

Fundamentalism was a retreat from everything perceived to threaten the bastions of what was understood to be true and orthodox.[8] Three major concerns occupied the fundamentalists in the years surrounding World War II. First was the influx of millions of immigrants and their various worldviews. Many of these were professing Roman Catholics, Lutherans, and Jews, none of whom shared the Puritan and revivalistic traditions of America and American evangelicalism. The second concern that occupied fundamentalists was the radical shift in contemporary thought, most famously evidenced by the Scopes Trial. The Scopes Trial typified such conflicts as the city versus the country, progress versus supposed ignorance, and most certainly modernism versus fundamentalism.

The trial itself revolved around a teacher who was charged and found guilty of violating the Tennessee antievolution law. Though fundamentalists "won" on the issue of evolution, some contend that the movement as a whole earned nothing but ridicule. This interpretation is based largely on the cross-examination of William Jennings Bryan by Scopes's attorney, Clarence Darrow, one of the most gifted attorneys in the nation. Bryan was unable to defend the Bible on the most simplistic points. As George Marsden has written, the trial brought an "outpouring of derision. The rural setting . . . stamped the entire movement with an indelible image," that of the anti-intellectual, Southern farmer.[9]

The third concern that occupied the fundamentalists was an approach to the Bible called higher criticism, an approach that was largely literary in nature and often began with a posture of skepticism: "Who really wrote this book of the Bible? Did that really happen the way the Bible says it did?" For fundamentalists, this criticism undermined the idea that the Bible was special revelation. Higher criticism was also associated with German liberalism in education and with Germany at the heart of both world wars during this era. It's no surprise that evangelist Billy Sunday quipped that if you turned hell upside down, you would find "Made in Germany" stamped on the bottom.[10]

In such a context, fundamentalists decided to enter into a holy war and began to equate their success with the future of Western civilization.[11] This strong and emotive response to these three concerns, along with countless others, formed what Thomas Kuhn calls a paradigm shift.[12] Kuhn argues that science progresses not through the accumulation of new "facts" but through "paradigm conflicts" that exist between divergent worldviews. When two perspectives use radically different models and presuppositions, communication breakdown and conflict are inevitable. Marsden notes that Kuhn's theory helped explain and clarify the fundamentalist experience during this time of American history.[13]

After the 1920s, fundamentalism entered into a period perhaps best termed a "retreat into institutionalization." Rather than engage culture, fundamentalists retreated and sought areas where they could control doctrine, education, and morals. This isolation, of course, did little to alter the currents of culture. But neither did the Religious Right to which it eventually gave birth.

Remembering the Religious Right

Many fundamentalists grew uneasy with the denominational separatism, social and cultural irresponsibility, and anti-intellectual stance that pervaded during the years of controversy with the modernists.[14] These individuals branched off and formed the movement now known as contemporary American evangelicalism, led by such men as Carl F. H. Henry, Harold Ockenga, and Billy Graham and giving birth to such entities as the National Association of Evangelicals, Fuller Theological Seminary, and *Christianity Today* magazine. This new coalition gained national attention in 1976 when Jimmy Carter, a Southern Baptist and professed born-again evangelical, was elected president of the United States. *Newsweek* magazine declared 1976 "The Year of the Evangelical."[15] This newfound prominence led to the desire among certain evangelicals to shape contemporary culture and values. This was largely attempted through the political realm. The late 1970s saw the formation of organizations, such as the Moral Majority, that would come to typify the emergence of a Christian Right, or conservative Christian political activity that became associated with contemporary American evangelicalism. Such groups organized evangelicals to support the 1980 election of Ronald Reagan to the presidency of the United States and to lend their voices to a host of issues, including school prayer, tuition tax credits, and the reversal of Supreme Court decisions such as *Roe v. Wade*, which legalized abortion.

Two concerns fueled this politicization. First was an obsession, bordering on paranoia, with what was called secular humanism. Popularized as a tremendous threat to the continuing existence of Christianity, secular humanism was generally defined as the idea that humanity does not answer to any higher authority than humanity itself. Inherent within this definition was the correlate that human beings are basically good or can become good by their own efforts. As a result, many evangelicals understood secular humanism as a means to decide what was good and then to motivate humanity toward that goal without reference to God.[16] The second concern that brought many evangelicals into the public arena was the vision of a Christian America, the idea that America was founded as a Christian nation and flourished under the benevolent hand of Divine Providence and that America's blessings would remain only as long as America was faithful to God as a nation.[17]

Of course, this movement of contemporary American evangelicalism to become more involved in the political realm was not terribly successful, at least in terms of the immediate goals. Yes, Reagan was elected—twice—with the subsequent Supreme Court appointments. But the wider culture remained unaffected. Not only is *Roe v. Wade* still on the books, but we've also added *Obergefell v. Hodges*, which legalized gay marriage. As David Brooks assesses our day, the simple reality is that "American culture is shifting away from orthodox Christian positions on homosexuality, premarital sex, contraception, out-of-wedlock childbearing, divorce and a range of other social issues."[18]

So if the fundamentalist approach did not work (becoming cloistered), and neither did that of the Religious Right (becoming combative), what will? Before we can engage that question, we must have a clear sense of what we mean by the word *culture* itself.

The Meaning of Culture

So what is culture?

As a professor of mine once opined during my graduate school years, culture is the world in which we are born and the world that is born in us. Or, put another way, the world in which we live and the world that lives in us, which means we are talking about *everything*. Culture is the comprehensive, penetrating context that encompasses life and thought, art and speech, entertainment and sensibility, values and faith. It cannot be reduced to that which is simply economic or political, demographic or technological. Going further, the essence of culture, in regard to its most profound challenge, is that it is a spirit, a perspective on the world. It doesn't simply give a context for our values; it *shapes* our values because it has values in and of itself. It doesn't just provide the atmosphere for something such as communication; it forms what communication *is* and how it is achieved. Culture alters not only what is said but also what is heard—and how.

Sociologist Clifford Geertz has written some of the most penetrating and insightful definitions related to culture, and he has concluded that culture is "thick," meaning it cannot be reduced to any one thing. Instead, it is an entire way of life. And, he adds, it is largely self-created. Culture is something we invent, create, and fashion. Geertz, borrowing from fellow sociologist Max Weber, notes that "man is an animal suspended in webs of significance he himself has spun." Geertz then adds, "I take culture to be those webs."[19]

I was struck by a quote I came across one day: "'I am the art in your art houses, the ideas in your institutions, the laws in your land, the message in your movies, the thoughts of your teachers, the values your kids value. I affect you. Do you affect me?'—Culture."[20]

The Meaning of Countercultural

As part of a project funded by the Hewlett Foundation, Michael Gerson and Peter Wehner interviewed a wide range of evangelical authors, academics, college presidents, and nonprofit leaders about the post-Christian cultural shift. "Without exception, the leaders we consulted believe evangelicals are at a pivot point in their relationship to American culture."[21] Those who once had power and influence, and have seen it slip away, feel fear and frustration. Usually, this is the older guard, many of whom were (or are) part of the Religious Right. Younger evangelicals have often met the change by retreating into an "apolitical Christian subculture." The idea is that simply living a life following Jesus will effect cultural change. Some have coined this the Benedict Option, named after Benedict of Nursia, who "inspired and organized a monastic alternative to the sins of ancient Rome." As Rod Dreher adds, the only answer is for Christians to "build resilient communities within our condition of internal exile."[22]

Gerson and Wehner are right when they take both approaches somewhat to task. "Instead of raging at the loss of influence or making grudging concessions to modernity," they write, "we might take this moment to display the essential character of Christianity—one that appeals and persuades outside the faith."[23] They take note of the work of Rodney Stark, a sociologist of religion, who has repeatedly detailed how the Jesus movement in the second and third centuries became the dominant faith of Western civilization (indeed, the world's largest religion). Stark points to the "communal compassion" and social networks of the early Christians as well as "their care for the sick, widows, and orphans; their welcoming of strangers and care for outsiders; their respect for women (who were considered second-class citizens); and their connection to non-Christians."[24]

I believe the so-called Benedict Option is not as far from this as Gerson and Wehner might think, however. As Dreher himself has written, "Given this post-Christian new 'dark age,' we . . . Christians must pioneer new ways to bind ourselves to Scripture, to our traditions, and to each other—not for mere survival, but so that the church can be the authentic light of Christ to a world lost in darkness."[25] If I might be so bold as to translate, our hope is for the church to be the church.

To be truly countercultural begins with being truly Christlike. We cannot convey anything related to the truth of Christ apart from reflecting Christ himself. As Gandhi once said, "I like your

Christ, I do not like your Christians. Your Christians are so unlike your Christ."[26] We often marvel at the growth of the early church, the explosion of faith in Christ in such numbers and speed that in only a blink of history, the Roman Empire officially turned from paganism to Christianity. We look for formulas and programs, services and processes. The simple truth is that the early Christians were very much like Jesus, so much so that the name Christian, meaning "little Christ," came into existence (Acts 11). Yes, as Michael Green has noted, they shared the gospel like it was gossip over the backyard fence.[27] But what did people find when they responded to the evangelical call? As Tertullian noted, the awed pagan reaction to the Christian communal life was, "How these Christians seem to love each other."[28]

God Looks Good on You

I recently read a line that caught my attention. One person said of another, "God looks good on you." The context made it clear that the line didn't mean God looked on them in a favorable way, as in God's attitude or spirit toward them, but that when people looked at their life, it made God look good. God should look good on us to others. God looked good on Jesus. I've always marveled at how Jesus could proclaim absolute truth without compromise to those far from God and then those very people would invite him to their parties. Yet, as I wrote in *The Rise of the Nones*, we're not quite pulling off the Jesus life.

Many of those outside the Christian faith think Christians no longer represent what Jesus had in mind—that Christianity in our society is not what it was meant to be. We're seen as hyperpolitical, out of touch, pushy in our beliefs, and arrogant. And the biggest perceptions of all are that we are homophobic, hypocritical, and judgmental. Simply put, in the minds of many people, modern-day Christianity no longer seems Christian.

For example, in a video that's been viewed over a million times on YouTube, songwriter and comedian Tim Minchin asks a Sydney, Australia, audience, "Are you up for a . . . sing?" Minchin begins to sing, "I love Jesus, I love Jesus." He prompts the audience to join him. "Who do you love? Sing it!" Soon the whole crowd is involved, singing, "I love Jesus, I love Jesus." Then Minchin changes the lyrics: "I love Jesus, I hate faggots, I love Jesus, I hate faggots." The crowd stops singing along.

Minchin looks up from his guitar as if he doesn't understand the nature of the problem. "What happened? I just lost you there," he says. After a halfhearted attempt to get the group singing again, he gives up. "Ah, well," he says, "maybe these are ideas best shared in churches."[29]

Much of that image has been earned. We've acted in ways, talked in ways, lived in ways that have stolen from God's reputation. All this and more has flowed from the research of Gabe Lyons and David Kinnaman on how people view the church and people in it. Here's the heart of what they found. Among young American "outsiders," the following words or phrases were offered as possible descriptors of Christianity. The number who affirmed their accuracy is also included.[30]

- antihomosexual (91%)
- judgmental (87%)
- hypocritical (85%)
- old-fashioned (78%)
- too involved in politics (75%)
- out of touch with reality (72%)
- insensitive to others (70%)
- boring (68%)
- not accepting of other faiths (64%)
- confusing (61%)

I commissioned a similar study in which researchers went to those who were unchurched and asked them a simple question: "How did the church and those inside it lose you?" I first published the results of the research, done in coordination with the Barna Research Group, in my book *Rethinking the Church*.[31] Comparing the two studies is interesting.

In my own earlier research, the unchurched gave the following reasons for abandoning the church:

- There is no value in attending (74%).
- Churches have too many problems (61%).
- I do not have the time (48%).
- I am simply not interested (42%).
- Churches ask for money too frequently (40%).
- Church services are usually boring (36%).
- Christian churches hold no relevance for the way I live (34%).
- I do not believe in God or I am unsure that God exists (12%).

Such findings pointed to a culture that was saying, "God, yes; church, no." Now research shows the deepening crisis, for it points to a culture that says, "God, perhaps; Christianity and Christians, no." The idea of even considering church is seemingly off the table. But not because those outside the church don't see value in the church. And not because the church itself, as the body of Christ, is not the hope of the world. The problem is the church is not being the church, much less a countercultural one. If we were, then God would begin to look good on us again—even if what we say is alien to every other voice the unchurched might be hearing.

People will often look at Mecklenburg Community Church and wonder what the attraction is to the unchurched. Spend a week with us and you'll see. There is unity and love among the attenders. Grace flows freely with truth as its banner. In the midst of family dysfunction, there is authentic community. You'll be challenged to join us in rescuing sex-trafficked young girls from the brothels in the Philippines, work with orphans in Argentina, and serve the working poor on our doorstep. You will be challenged to consider having Christ intersect the deepest needs of your life and then grow deep in that relationship. You will be confronted with the reality of having one and only one life and then making that life count.

It's infectious.

How the Irish Saved Civilization

But being countercultural by fleshing out the life of Christ is not enough if the understanding of that life of Christ is devoid of the attempt to actively influence the post-Christian culture. Being countercultural is more about how best to exert that influence. In 1995, Thomas Cahill came out with the provocatively titled book *How the Irish Saved Civilization*. "Ireland," contends Cahill,

> had one moment of unblemished glory. . . . As the Roman Empire fell, as all through Europe matted, unwashed barbarians descended on the Roman cities, looting artifacts and burning books, the Irish, who were just learning to read and write, took up the great labor of copying all of Western literature.[32]

Then missionary-minded Irish monks brought what had been preserved on their isolated island back to the continent, refounding European civilization. And that, Cahill concludes, is how the Irish saved civilization.

But there is more at hand in Cahill's study than meets the eye. Cahill notes that, beyond the loss of Latin literature and the development of the great national European literatures that an illiterate Europe would not have established, something else would have perished in the West: "The habits of the mind that encourage thought." Why would this matter? Cahill continues his assessment: "And when Islam began its medieval expansion, it would have encountered scant resistance to its plans—just scattered tribes of animists, ready for a new identity." Without a robust mind to engage the onslaught—and a Christian one at that—the West would have been under the crescent instead of the cross.[33]

Never before have the habits of the mind mattered more. As Winston Churchill presciently stated in his address to Harvard University in 1943, "The empires of the future will be empires of the mind." Oxford theologian Alister McGrath, reflecting on Churchill's address, noted that Churchill's point was that a great transition was taking place in Western culture with immense implications for all who lived in it. The powers of the new world would not be nation-states, as with empires past, but ideologies. Ideas, not nations, would captivate and conquer in the future. The starting point for the conquest of the world would now be the human mind.[34] Or as John Stott once proclaimed, "We may talk of 'conquering' the world for Christ. But what sort of 'conquest' do we mean? Not a victory by force of arms. . . . This is a battle of ideas."[35]

Yet as I wrote in *A Mind for God*, there are surprisingly few warriors. Those who follow Christ have too often retreated into personal piety and good works. Or as one BBC commentator I heard on the radio while jogging one morning in Oxford said, Christians have too often offered mere "feelings" and "philanthropy." Speaking specifically to the challenge from Islam, he added that what is needed is more "hard thinking" applied to the issues of the day.

Which is why finding our cultural voice is more pressing than ever.

Discussion Questions

1. At the beginning of this chapter, you read the following quote from John Stott referring to the teachings of Jesus: "If the

church realistically accepted his standards and values . . . and lived by them, it would be the alternative society he always intended it to be, and would offer to the world an authentic Christian counter-culture." Does that spark anything in you that has been missing for some time?

2. In your life and ministry, how do you feel the vision of the church is perceived by those around you? How does that view differ from Jesus's own vision for the church?

3. The church's mission, according to the Bible, involves active evangelism with subsequent discipleship, coupled with strategic service to those in need. Which part of that mission is your ministry lacking? Which part are you actively working on?

4. Do you think the church acting as the church is a barrier or a blessing to Generation Z? Why do you feel this way?

5. The church is supposed to be a counterculture that is different from anything around it. That involves not being isolated from society and not conforming to society. Do you or your church tend toward one of the two? What can you do this year to move toward becoming a true counterculture in the way the Bible explains it?

6. Culture is the world in which we live and the world that lives in us. It doesn't simply give a context for our values; it *shapes* our values because it has values in and of itself. Does this mesh with your previous understanding of culture? If not, what does this definition cause you to think about that you may have been missing?

7. We cannot convey anything related to the truth of Christ apart from reflecting Christ himself. Be honest with yourself. Are there areas of your life or your ministry that are not reflecting Christ? What can you do to change that starting today?

5

Finding Our Voice

For the word of God is alive and active. Sharper than any double-edged sword, it penetrates even to dividing soul and spirit, joints and marrow; it judges the thoughts and attitudes of the heart.

Hebrews 4:12

The pastor of a large and influential church was recently asked about his stance on gay marriage. He gave what I thought was a very astute response. He said that in regard to such matters, there are three things that must be considered: "There's the world we live in, there's the weight we live with, and there's the Word we live by."[1]

That's actually quite right.

Consider the world we live in. Its position on gay marriage has changed seismically over the last few years. Churches have never failed to have the moral high ground on this matter . . . until now. Our voice, as Christians, is clearly a minority report in the modern world.

Consider the weight we live with. Who isn't heartbroken that people of any orientation or lifestyle, color or creed are bullied, discriminated against, hated, or terrorized? Speaking to the issue of gay marriage in a manner that would consciously add in any way to such repugnant behavior would be unconscionable.

But then we must consider the Word we live by. By this he meant, "What the Bible says." Where the Bible stands, we must stand.

Then came the awkward moment. The pastor continued, saying, "It would be much easier if you could feel like all of those three just easily lined up. But they don't necessarily. . . . The real issues in people's lives are too important for us to just reduce it down to a 'yes' or 'no' answer in a media outlet."[2]

Now before you rush to a cry of "Compromise!" he's once again actually right. First, they don't line up. At all. Second, anyone who works with people—I mean, really works with people—knows that there is a serious pastoral side to such issues. Making simple declarations of your stance at conferences filled with the already convinced does not represent the real world. Nor are these declarations particularly helpful to those we are trying to reach. To give an answer that truly serves the historic Christian position on such an issue takes more than a tweet. Further, when we are being asked such a question in a secular context, we must be even more careful with our answer.

Why? Because there is a thin line between maintaining an earned voice through which to speak to culture and compromising the very message we long to share. There are certain things we know we can say that will shut the other side down. And we don't want to shut the other side down. But we don't want to compromise either. So when dealing with the secular world, we pick our way through such conundrums with care. Never lying, never compromising, but picking our battles—answering in ways that let us maintain a voice so that we can continue to have listening ears when it's time to express the voice of challenge.

I'll give you a somewhat less controversial example. If you were to ask me, point blank, if I had a denominational heritage, I would answer "Baptist." But I don't lead with "Baptist." I lead with "Christ follower." And when asked about the church I pastor, Mecklenburg Community Church, I lead with "interdenominational" and stress that we have people from all backgrounds, including no church background at all. While I hold to such classic theological tenets as congregational participation, believer's baptism by immersion, and biblical inerrancy, the tag "Baptist" is one of the more pejorative, jarring, discomfiting labels around. For reasons, I might add, that have more to do with social and cultural missteps by various leaders than its actual theological and ecclesiastical sinew. Yet there is little doubt that our theology is clearly baptistic.

Choosing his battles wisely is something Jesus did masterfully. He refused to get pulled into Roman politics, even when baited. He didn't rise to many of the theological squabbles among the Jews. But when he did, it was always for something significant. Like the debate between the Pharisees and the Sadducees concerning the resurrection; to Jesus, that one mattered.

So returning to our pastor, should his be the model response to a question on gay marriage? With respect, no—because the nature of marriage and family lies at the heart of the created order, and the nature of sexual expression lies at the heart of physical morality. The third leg of the cultural conundrum, following the world we live in and the weight we live with, is the Word we live by. And when we consider the Word, we find that it does offer a concrete position. Its response to whether gay marriage is acceptable, no matter how much we might need to explain such a response, is a simple no. And to his credit, the pastor in question later added a clarifying word: "My personal view on the subject of homosexuality would line up with most traditionally held Christian views. I believe the writings of Paul are clear on this subject."[3] But as Jonathan Merritt rightly pointed out in covering the matter, "In a moment when so much is at stake a non-statement statement is, well, quite a statement."[4]

Yes, it is.

And that is the challenge we all face in finding our voice culturally, specifically in speaking to Generation Z. As detailed earlier, members of Generation Z hold few things dearer than acceptance and inclusivity. They view many moral stances, such as opposing gay marriage, as social stances in line with racism. To them, acceptance means affirmation. If you don't affirm, you don't accept. This unfortunately permeates all of culture, not just Generation Z, where to be considered welcoming to, say, the LGBT community, is code for condoning their lifestyle.

So what kind of "voice" should we use?

Three Voices

Biblically, there are three primary voices speaking into culture: the prophetic, the evangelistic, and the heretical. The prophetic voice, such as Jeremiah's, is clear in its denunciations and warnings. The prophetic voice is an admonishing one, a "thou shalt not," a clarion call to turn to God and get right with God. It is not a popular voice for culture to hear. That is why it is not a popular voice for Christians to use. Quick, name a popular prophet. See? As an old seminary professor of mine once quipped, "Assume a prophet's voice, expect a prophet's reward."

The second voice is the evangelistic voice. This is the apostle Paul standing on Mars Hill (Acts 17). It is the voice attempting to build bridges across cultural divides, to explain things, to make apologetic cases. The evangelistic voice is focused on calling people to a relationship with Christ as Forgiver and Leader.

The final voice is the heretical voice. To be sure, heretical voices in the Bible are never celebrated, but they are noted. The false prophets of the Old Testament and the false teachers of the New Testament are frequently detailed. As the apostle Peter declared, "There will be false teachers among you. They will secretly introduce destructive heresies" (2 Pet. 2:1). This is the voice that not only speaks against the gospel but also, more specifically, attempts to distort the gospel's presentation to culture itself.

The heretical voice is most at play and seems to be the most seductive for Christian leaders when attempting to engage culture. Nearly forty years ago, writing about the challenges of communicating the message of Christ in the twentieth century, John R. W. Stott wrote of the three chief obstacles facing preaching: "the anti-authority mood makes people unwilling to listen, addiction of television makes them unable to do so, and the contemporary atmosphere of doubt makes many preachers both unwilling and unable to speak. Thus there is a paralysis at both ends, in the speaking and in the hearing."[5] It is precisely in the "speaking" end of things that we must not lose focus.

It is tempting to try to connect with a post-Christian culture by mirroring its post-Christian values and sentiments. For example, Rob Bell, former pastor and frequent guest on Oprah Winfrey's said television network, maintains that a church that doesn't support same-sex marriage is irrelevant. Bell earlier questioned the existence of hell in his 2011 book *Love Wins*. Bell made the comments about gay marriage on an episode of Winfrey's *Super Soul Sunday*, where he appeared with his wife to talk about religion and spirituality. He called the church's acceptance of gay marriage "inevitable" and the reason that it should be accepted is because loneliness "is not good for the world."

"I think culture is already there," Bell continued, "and the church will continue to be even more irrelevant when it quotes letters from 2,000 years ago as their best defense."[6] His thinking is that for the church to be relevant, it must not only embrace homoerotic behavior but also jettison Scripture as any kind of authoritative guide in regard to this or (seemingly) any other cultural issue in which public opinion goes against Scripture. The new source of revelation is personal fulfillment. In this case, no one should be lonely, so whatever fills the loneliness gap should be affirmed.

We must understand the danger of such an approach. Yes, it landed Bell on television. Yes, it was and is a popular stance culturally. But if the Bible is to be cavalierly abandoned as mere "letters from 2,000 years ago," then historic orthodoxy has truly been abandoned. Christians embrace the Old Testament as inspired by God because Jesus did, and the New Testament as equally sacred because it is based on the teaching of Jesus and his apostles. If we relegate the Bible to less than the revelation of God, then we are relegating Jesus to less than the Son of God. As Christians, we can have robust discussions on the nature of inspiration, and certainly on the dynamics of interpretation, but not on the authority of the Bible itself. That was established by Jesus.

Further, to adopt self-fulfillment and self-satisfaction as the ultimate apologetic is to make the self central to all things. This was, of course, the great temptation put before Adam and Eve in the garden that led to the fall of humanity. Pursuing whatever we desire is not what is best for the world. What is best for the world is when we submit our desires to what is best for the world. And that is determined by God.

Finally, the "relevance" of the church is not found in its capitulation to culture but in its transformation of culture. Any student of ecclesiastical history knows that whenever orthodoxy was abandoned in order for the church to mirror culture, it led to the church's great demise. We do not gain the world's attention through a compromised voice but through a prophetic one. No one would argue the need for a winsome and compelling voice for Christ in our culture more than I; no one would argue the need for contrition for a lack of love toward those with a same-sex orientation more than I; no one would argue the need for the church's relevance more than I. But if we follow Bell's strategy, the church really will continue to be even more irrelevant than it already is.

Why?

Because it will cease to be the church.

The key in attempting to speak into culture with relevance, but not compromise, is found in the dynamic between translation and transformation. Theologian Millard Erickson, building on the insights of William E. Hordern, notes that every generation must *translate* the gospel into its unique cultural context. But this is very different from *transforming* the message of the gospel into something that was never intended by the biblical witness.[7] Transformation of the message must be avoided at all costs. *Translation*, however, is essential for a winsome and compelling presentation of the gospel of Christ. It is precisely this interplay between translation and transformation that must be navigated by every leader in regard to culture. If transformation takes place, then we have simply abandoned orthodoxy for the hopeful sake of warm bodies, and the tickling of ears does not exactly have a welcome spot in the biblical materials. If translation takes place, we intentionally build bridges of cultural understanding but retain our prophetic voice in the marketplace of ideas.

Transformation is heresy.

Translation is the heart of our mission.

Knowing the difference is the crucible of leadership and the difference between being in the world and being of the world.

I've always found pastors and church leaders visiting Mecklenburg for the first time interesting, particularly in what they say about the message. The most common refrain is, "You talk about heaven and hell, sin and the cross more than we do!" Perhaps we do. But that's the point. When discussing the truths of Scripture, it's not about what we say but how we say it. It's not about watering anything down but communicating it in a way that is winsome and compelling, relatable and identifiable. My goal is to take the language of culture and use it to convey the gospel of Christ—not in a way that changes the gospel but in a way that communicates it.

Learning the Prophetic Voice

History teaches that significant cultural change has always been born on the wings of oratory, whether the simple words offered in the "Gettysburg Address" on the field of battle in Pennsylvania or the soaring rhetoric of the "I Have a Dream" speech delivered on the steps of the Lincoln Memorial. This has certainly been the case for all great movements of the Holy Spirit that have impacted society, for preaching has always been in the vanguard of Christianity's engagement with contemporary culture. As John R. W. Stott has suggested, the art of preaching truly stands "between two worlds": the world of the biblical text and the modern world to which we bring those words to bear.[8]

The distinctive form of address espoused by the prophets was "thus says the Lord." Christopher J. H. Wright suggests that there were four principal prohibitions God expressed to Israel that were cultural in nature: idolatry, perversion, that which was destructive of persons, and callousness to the poor.[9] For example, digging deeper into one of these—perversion—we find that immorality was consistently condemned by the prophetic voice of the Old Testament. Such practices as prostitution, homosexuality, bestiality, and incest were denounced. God gave clear directions to Moses for the Israelites that they should "not do as they do in Egypt, where you used to live, and you must not do as they do in the land of Canaan, where I am bringing you" (Lev. 18:3). For example, God directed the Israelites, "Do not have sexual relations with an animal and defile yourself with it. . . . That is a perversion" (Lev. 18:23). Then God added, "Do not defile yourselves in any of these ways, because that is how the nations that I am going to drive out before you became defiled" (Lev. 18:24).

Today few want to use the prophetic voice. In fact, it is often seen as undermining the evangelistic voice. Many believe that the popularity and success of Billy Graham were due, in large part, to the fact that he kept his evangelistic voice and did not fall into a prophetic voice. In like manner, I've often heard pastors, particularly of large churches, say they do not want to speak out on the issues of the day for the sake of keeping their focus on the gospel and not alienating people on the front end. But this is a gross misunderstanding of not only Graham but also evangelism itself. Graham took stands against racism and many other social ills of his day, often at great personal cost. He was an evangelist, to be sure, but the lesson he learned was not to avoid social issues but to avoid politics. In fact, his involvement in politics early on in his ministry, particularly with Richard Nixon, proved to be one of his greatest regrets.

Yet the temptation to mute the prophetic voice is strong. As noted, some are tempted to believe that speaking out against a homoerotic lifestyle is counterproductive to gaining the listening ear of a culture that has embraced that very lifestyle. So, the thinking goes, let's drop the prophetic voice because of its cultural disdain in order to maximize the evangelistic voice for the sake of the gospel. And, as also noted, some would even take up the heretical voice and offer support to the homosexual lifestyle.

The dilemma is that without the prophetic voice, there is no gospel. Without a sense of the true nature of our sin condition, which demands an understanding of sin itself, there is no good news. Without the prophetic voice, the evangelistic voice is mere sentimentality. Or worse, just cheap grace. Grace is only amazing when we realize how much we are in need of it. To be sure, the prophetic voice without the winsome and compelling heart of evangelism is just strident condemnation. We need both voices. But in our day, it is not the loss of the evangelistic voice I fear but the prophetic one. And even more dire is the increasing use of the heretical voice in the name of amplifying the evangelistic one.

What we need is the most powerful voice of all, which is, of course, the Bible's. If we teach the Bible as the very Word of God, then we have unleashed revelation itself. God has broken out into the world in blinding flashes of lightning, and the Bible records the thunder. As a result, we can only bow our heads and open our hearts, minds, and hands. Revelation is different from something merely good or helpful; it is the voice of God echoing down from heaven. It demands that we become like clay—malleable and shaped. If we harden ourselves against revelation's voice, then again, like clay, we can only crumble in response to its touch.

Not simply in practice but in thought.

As Mark Galli wrote in an editorial in *Christianity Today*:

> The Bible is the Word of God primarily because it reveals the nature of God—who God is and what he has done for us. And that in turn shows us what it means to be those created in his image. Yes, it includes practical teaching for daily living. But most . . . pastors, teachers, and small-group leaders would be wise to spend more energy showing how the Bible is the source of the great church doctrines—which are so often about God and his saving work. It's time for our main pedagogical question to be not, "What difference does this make?" but "What does this tell us about our good God?"[10]

Sadly, most teach the Bible as a good book or a self-help manual. They fear tapping into its deepest voice, and deepest waters, for fear of turning people away. Yet it's only the Bible's true voice that will offer the world what it doesn't already have.

And most desperately needs.

Ready for an irony?

I find that most people, particularly men, want to be challenged in regard to their deepest held views and convictions. They want to grapple with their opinions and thoughts, perspectives and ideologies. They like to wrestle with another mind, another view, another perspective—if, however, it's done in a way that makes it a fair match. The prophetic voice is declarative, to be sure, but it is also inviting. It invites people to engage their somewhat settled views with a variant viewpoint.

But first we have to get past the initial response.

A Culture of Offense

Make no mistake: using the prophetic voice will cause offense, particularly in what is increasingly an "offense" culture. In a cover article for the *Atlantic* titled "The Coddling of the American Mind," authors Greg Lukianoff and Jonathan Haidt explore how in the name of "emotional well-being" college students are increasingly demanding protection from words and ideas they don't like and seeking punishment of those who give even accidental offense. "A movement is arising . . . to scrub campuses clean of words, ideas, and subjects that might cause discomfort or give offense."[11]

Two terms loom large on today's campuses. First is *microaggressions*. These are small actions or word choices that "seem on their face to have no malicious intent but that are thought of as a kind of violence nonetheless." The second term is *trigger warnings*. This is what a professor is expected to issue "if something in a course might cause a strong emotional response."

During the 2014–15 school year, the deans and department chairs at the ten University of California system schools were presented by administrators at faculty leader-training sessions with examples of microaggressions. The list of offensive statements included "America is the land of opportunity" and "I believe the most qualified person should get the job." As Lukianoff and Haidt note, this is beyond political correctness. The ultimate aim, it seems, is to turn campuses into "safe spaces" where "young adults are shielded from words and ideas that make some uncomfortable . . . [and] this movement seeks to punish anyone who interferes with that aim."[12]

Ready for another term? Try *vindictive protectiveness*.

In essence, in the name of emotional well-being, students can eliminate anything they do not want to think about, read about, or be challenged about. And penalize those who would expose them to it.

How?

In the name of "offense."

"Emotional reasoning dominates many campus debates and discussions," write Lukianoff and Haidt. "A claim that someone's words are 'offensive' is not just an expression of one's own subjective feeling of offendedness. It is, rather, a public charge that the speaker has done something objectively wrong."[13] For example, a student at Indiana University–Purdue read a book titled *Notre Dame vs. the Klan*, a book that honored student opposition to the Ku Klux Klan when students marched on Notre Dame in 1924. The cover of the book featured a picture of a Klan rally. Despite the book's actual content, the student was found guilty of racial harassment by the university's Affirmative Action Office.

Or consider "Hump Day" at the University of St. Thomas in Minnesota. Inspired by Wednesday being known as hump day in the workweek, students were going to be allowed to see and pet a camel. But a group of students created a Facebook group protesting the event for animal cruelty, for being a waste of money, and for being insensitive to people from the Middle East (despite the event being devoid of any reference to Middle Eastern peoples). The event was canceled because the "program [was] dividing people and would make for an uncomfortable and possible unsafe environment." All to say, the "thin argument 'I'm offended' becomes an unbeatable trump card." This is breeding a generation to "focus on small or accidental slights" and, even more, to then "relabel the people who have made such remarks as aggressors."[14]

Imagine if the offense was not "micro" but "macro," as the Bible's most penetrating statements most certainly are. Which means that if we use the prophetic voice, we will have enemies. A lot of enemies. This isn't a popular idea. Many Christians seem more intent on fitting into culture, or at least getting its affirmation, than opposing it. And the entire idea of being an enemy, or having one, seems out of sync with the Christ life.

But it isn't.

Jesus made it very clear that he did not come to bring peace but a sword (and rumor has it his own life did not end in a crowning but in a crucifying). The apostle Paul talked about open spiritual warfare in his letter to the Ephesians. The Bible speaks plainly about the "god" of this fallen world, and it is Satan himself.

So why is there such a great temptation for Christians today to opt for a popular stance instead of a prophetic one? For many, there is a bitter taste in their mouths from the caustic and abrasive era of the Moral Majority and the Religious Right, so much so that they have overcompensated by not wanting to be seen as condemning anything. For others, it is spiritual insecurity. Somehow they are not "legitimate" until they are embraced by MTV or fawned over by *Slate*. It is as if our model is Bono—be a cultural rock star while espousing a nonoffensive Christian faith. Not to denigrate Bono, whose faith is sincere and who has worked tirelessly for AIDS orphans around the world, but the better model would be Bonhoeffer, someone who clearly saw the lines of good and evil and worked tirelessly to overthrow evil (in his case, Hitler and the Third Reich). Rather than gaining popularity, Dietrich Bonhoeffer experienced execution at a concentration camp.

Suffice it to say, we are behind enemy lines. When behind enemy lines, there are enemies. The goal is not to be enemy-free, as if Christianity at its purest is so winsome and compelling that no one who "gets it" will ever reject it. No, the gospel is scandalous and offensive. Many will openly reject it, not to mention its moral mandates. We are not to embody culture but the Christian *coun-*terculture. The kingdom of God we advance is not the kingdom currently in place.

The problem isn't having enemies. It's having the right ones and for the right reasons. Don't have enemies because you are intentionally offensive in spirit and interrelational dynamics. Don't have enemies because you are caustic and abrasive. Don't have enemies because you are unfeeling and unloving.

But . . .

Do have enemies because you stand for truth. Do have enemies because you will not waver in the face of majority opinion when it crashes against biblical authority. Do have enemies because you will not personally compromise your convictions.

After all, Jesus did.

Would Martin Luther King Jr. Be Heard Today?

Journalist Sharon Shahid once openly wondered whether Martin Luther King Jr.'s famed essay "Letter from Birmingham Jail" "would have made such a lasting impression or had as powerful an impact if today's instant communication devices existed, and if someone smuggled a BlackBerry or a mobile phone into his cell. What would have happened if he texted the famous letter or used Twitter—in 140 characters or fewer?"

"Instead of a legacy," she suggests, "he most likely would have started a conversation."

And that's all.

"King's voice—so poignant and crystal-clear in print—simply would lose its resonance in cyber ink. . . . A tweet would have faded into ether minutes after it was released, drowned out by a thousand other disparate musings."[15] But that is the least of the challenges King's words would face from our current context.

Why?

His was a prophet's voice based on a thoroughgoing Christian worldview.

And today there are few such prophets.

Consider the term itself, *worldview*, from the German *Weltanschauung* (literally, "world perception"), which suggests more than a set of ideas by which we judge other ideas. It is, as Gene Edward Veith has written, "a way to engage constructively the whole range of human expression from a Christian perspective."[16]

Or as Jonathan Edwards, arguably the greatest intellect America has ever produced, once contended, the basic goal of any intellect is to work toward "the consistency and agreement of our ideas with the ideas of God."[17]

Now consider the worldview questions posed by Charles Colson and Nancy Pearcey based on creation, the fall, and redemption: Where did we come from and who are we? What has gone wrong with the world? What can we do to fix it? How now shall we live?[18] Reflect on the response to the first and most foundational of these questions—Where did we come from? There are a limited number of answers at our disposal: we came about by chance (the naturalist contention); we don't really exist (the Hindu response); or, we were spoken into existence by God. If one makes the even more obscure suggestion that we were seeded here by another race of beings from another planet, as suggested by Cambridge physicist Stephen Hawking, one would then have to account for *their* existence.

So, for the Christian, the answer to "Where did we come from and who are we?" gives a foundation for thinking that no other answer gives. Because we were created, there is value in each person. There is meaning and purpose to every life. There is Someone above and outside our existence who stands over it as authority. Because of this answer, Martin Luther King Jr. could write the immortal words found in his jailhouse correspondence:

> There are two types of law: just and unjust. . . . A just law is a man-made code that squares with the moral law or the law of God. An unjust law is a code that is out of harmony with the moral law. . . . Any law that uplifts human personality is just. Any law that degrades human personality is unjust. All segregation statutes are unjust because segregation distorts the soul and damages the personality.[19]

King's argument was based on the worth of a human being bestowed by God regardless of what other humans might have to say; King laid claim to a law above man's law. No other worldview would have given King the basis for such a claim.

And from such a worldview, the world was changed.

But would such a worldview get a hearing today?

Only if it, too, was rooted in a prophetic voice.

Discussion Questions

1. When dealing with the secular world, it is wisest to approach sensitive topics with care. Never lying, never compromising, but picking our battles. The goal is to answer in ways that allow us to continue earning a voice in people's lives that will one day result in the opportunity for direct challenge to their worldview, but only when the time is right. Does that approach align with yours? If not, how do the two differ?

2. Generation Z views moral stances, such as opposing gay marriage, as social stances on par with racism. Does that shock you? Do you know how to approach such topics in light of their views?

3. Honestly evaluate your ministry. Are you treating the Bible as the Word of God, with all that entails, or are you treating it as something different from or less than that?

4. The relevance of the church is not found in its capitulation to culture but in its transformation of culture. Does that convict you in any way? If so, what about your church should change?

5. Every generation must translate the gospel into its unique setting without transforming the message itself. If an average none from Generation Z were to sit in your service this Sunday, would the experience make any sense to them? If not, how can you work to translate elements of the service so that the service connects with them without compromising the truth it contains?

6. Which voice, the prophetic, the evangelistic, or the heretical, is most prominent in your church? Assuming it's not the heretical, what can you do to introduce elements of the missing voice while maintaining a strong call to God's revealed truth?

7. When you think about your life, are you interested in being accepted and being safe? Are you interested in fitting in and keeping quiet? What problems does that present considering the mission of the church?

6

Rethinking Evangelism

Insanity: doing the same thing over and over again and expecting different results.

Albert Einstein

At this point in the journey, I am hopeful it is abundantly clear that approaches to evangelism used in the past must be ruthlessly reevaluated in light of the nature of a post-Christian culture and the generation it has spawned. The most foundational rethinking is one that in previous writings and in multiple settings I've sketched out to try to persuade pastors and church leaders of one foundational dynamic: the importance of process.

And I would like to sketch this out again here (see fig. 6.1).[1]

Let's set up a line with a scale from 1 to 10. We will set as a "1" any individual without knowledge of, or relationship with, Christ. And at a "10" is any individual who has made the decision to cross the line of faith and enter into a relationship with Christ.

Figure 6.1

1	10
No Relationship	Saving Faith in Christ

Using this scale, I want to look at these individuals, and culture as a whole, and contrast the year 1960 with what we find today. In thinking about the unchurched person living in the United States in 1960, I believe that I could reasonably argue that these beliefs would have been typical for them:

- an acceptance of the deity of Christ
- a belief that truth exists and that the Bible is trustworthy
- a positive image of the church and its leaders
- a church background and experience that were relatively healthy
- a foundational knowledge of the essential truths of the Christian faith
- a built-in sense of guilt or conviction that kicked in when they violated the basic tenets of the Judeo-Christian value system

Given all of this, I would place this person at an "8" in terms of their readiness to engage with and respond to the gospel (see fig. 6.2).

Figure 6.2
1960

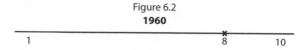

1	8	10

All it would take to move them from an 8 to a 10 (crossing the line of faith) was a bump. This made the evangelistic strategies of the 1960s—door-to-door visitation, Sunday school, church revivals and busing—extremely successful for the day. Evangelism was very "event" oriented, and the presentation of the Gospel and the message of salvation were often all it took for someone to cross the line of faith. I've often joked that if I were to meet a non-Christian like this I could get them to Jesus with a tweet!

If it has not already, the church needs to quickly come to the realization that strategies like these are no longer effective, because today so many people in our post-Christian culture are not just simply unchurched but solidly in the none category. Or they are a part of the squishy center discussed earlier that is moving decidedly to the left. And if they are a part of Generation Z, they are further removed from even a memory of the gospel. Today, the typical unchurched person on our scale would most likely fall at a "3" (see fig. 6.3).

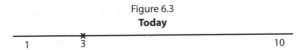

Figure 6.3
Today

| 1 | 3 | 10 |

The church must rethink evangelism—no longer can we be simply event driven. The church must view evangelism as both a process *and* an event. Because we are not dealing with an unchurched culture resting at an 8 (with a relatively advanced spiritual knowledge) but instead with a post-Christian unchurched culture resting at a 3, we must pay fresh attention to the *process* that leads people *to* the event of salvation. The goal is not simply knowing how to articulate the means of coming to Christ (when they move to a 10) but knowing how to facilitate and enable the person to progress up our scale from a 3 to a 7 or an 8, where they are able to even consider accepting Christ in a meaningful way.

Echoing this sentiment, in a rather obscure essay on modern man and his categories of thought, C. S. Lewis argued that when the gospel first broke out, the evangelistic task was essentially to one of three groups: Jews, Judaizing Gentiles, or pagans. All three believed in the supernatural. All were conscious of sin and feared divine judgment. Each offered some form of personal purification and release. They all believed the world had once been better than it now was. But now, Lewis argued, the average person shares none of those marks. In fact, he ended the essay by stating, "I sometimes wonder whether we shall not have to re-convert men to real Paganism as a preliminary to converting them to Christianity."[2]

Acts 2 versus Acts 17

So what does this situation mean practically? The heart of any evangelistic process is going to have to major in explanation. *Everything* must be explained, from music to messages, symbols to ritual, because so little is understood.

Let me suggest a biblical paradigm I have attempted to convey throughout my writings in recent years in relation to this rethinking. Biblically, it is as if we have moved from an Acts 2 cultural context to an Acts 17 cultural context.

In Acts 2, Peter is before the God-fearing Jews of Jerusalem. Here, in essence, was his message: "You know about the creation, Adam and Eve, and the fall; you know about Abraham and the chosen people of Israel; you know about Moses and the law; you know about the prophets and the promised coming of the Messiah. So we don't need to waste time on all that. What you need to know is that Jesus was that Messiah, you rejected him and killed him, and he rose again and unleashed his church, which means you need to repent."

It wasn't even the length of a good blog.

Result? Three thousand repented! Peter was able to speak to a group of people who were already monotheists, who already bought into the Old Testament Scriptures, and who already believed in a coming Messiah.

Now move forward to Acts 17, featuring Paul on Mars Hill speaking to the philosophers and spiritual seekers of Athens. Here was a spiritual marketplace where truth was relative, worldviews and gods littered the landscape, and the average person wouldn't know the difference between Isaac and an iPad. Paul knew he wasn't in Jerusalem anymore. So he didn't take an Acts 2 approach, much less give an Acts 2 message. He had to find a new way to connect with the culture and the people in it.

Paul surveyed the cultural landscape and found a touchstone—an altar to an unknown God. The culture was so pluralistic that the only thing people could agree on was that you couldn't know anything for sure. "What if I could tell you that God's name? Would that be of interest?" Paul began. He then went all the way back to creation and began to work his way forward—laying a foundation for an understanding and acceptance of the gospel.

Different culture, different approach.

This is precisely where we find ourselves today. We are not speaking to the God-fearing Jews in Jerusalem. We are standing on Mars Hill and need an Acts 17 mindset with an Acts 17 strategy. Which means our primary cultural currency is going to need to be explanation. It's not enough to move from a King James Version of the Bible to Eugene Peterson's uber-contemporary paraphrase *The Message* in our speaking. We have to begin by saying, "This is a Bible. It has sixty-six books. There's an Old Testament and a New Testament. It tells the story of us and God."

And then we need to explain that story.

This was driven home to me through the 2013 movie *Gravity* about an astronaut, played by George Clooney, and a medical engineer, played by Sandra Bullock, who work together in an effort to survive after a catastrophe destroys their shuttle and leaves them adrift in orbit. It was a critically acclaimed, special-effects spectacular.

But I was taken by one scene in particular, a moment when the character played by Bullock felt she was going to die. Her character, Ryan Stone, speaks the following words through her tears to the emptiness of space:

> Oh, I'm going to die . . . I know . . . we're all gonna die, everybody knows that. But I'm going to die today! It's funny that . . . you know, to know. But the thing is, is that I'm still scared. I'm

111

really scared. No one will mourn for me, no one will pray for my soul. Will you mourn for me? Will you say a prayer for me? Or is it too late?

Ugh. I mean, I'd say one for myself, but I've never prayed in my life, so. . .

But nobody ever taught me how. Nobody ever taught me how.[3]

That scene has haunted me ever since I first saw it. No one ever taught her to pray. No one explained it.

But someone could have.

The Curse of Knowledge

So why don't people explain? Much of the problem rests with what has been called the curse of knowledge.

Try something. Tap out the beats to "Happy Birthday" with your hand on a desk or chair or whatever is handy where you are reading this. You're singing the song in your head while tapping out the beats with your hand or fingers. It takes only a few seconds.

Okay, once you do it, ask yourself, "Do I think most people would guess the song based on my beats?" It's such a familiar song that, if you're like most people, you probably imagine they would have.

This was an actual experiment conducted at Stanford University. Researchers found that listeners were able to guess a song right only about 2.5 percent of the time—getting three songs out of about one hundred twenty. But here's what's interesting. The person tapping thought those listening were getting it right at least 90 percent of the time. So the listeners were getting the song right only one time out of forty, but the tapper thought they were getting it right one time out of every two.

The difference was that the tapper was hearing the song in their head. When they were tapping, they couldn't imagine the other person not hearing the song in the background. This is called the curse of knowledge. Once we know something, we find it hard to imagine what it's like not to know it.[4]

Have you forgotten what it's like to be apart from Christ?

The world needs you to remember.

We're so used to talking to the already convinced that we have lost our intuitive sense of what it means to talk to someone who isn't a Christ follower. I assume no knowledge whatsoever. I never use terms such as *Trinity, revelation, sin,* or *grace* without explaining what they mean. Even something as elemental as how I reference a passage in the Bible is explanatory in nature. Instead of saying, "This passage is from John 1:14," I say something along the lines of, "This is from the biography of Jesus written by John, one of our four biographies in the Bible."

As much as I consider myself sensitized to this as the pastor of a church with over 70 percent of its growth from the unchurched, I still get startling reminders that keep me on my toes, such as this response from a woman following an email about an upcoming celebration of the Lord's Supper:

> Thanks for the informative email. I have been going to Meck for about a month now and I love it! I have even talked my two friends into joining. We are all thankful to be part of an awesome church with great values. I do have one question. I remember hearing about . . . [an upcoming] celebration of the Lord's Supper. What does that mean? . . . What is a celebration of the Lord's Supper? Does that mean we all bring some kind of food to share? I am planning on going . . . but I wanted to make sure I bring something if need be. Any information you can provide . . . would be greatly appreciated!

Such illiteracy is not confined to biblical knowledge; it involves the dynamics of spiritual life itself. I have to show how a life that follows Christ is actually marked by that following. This means I have to apply the Bible's teaching to life's most pressing challenges, conflicts, and choices. The goal is to illustrate what a Christ follower would do or think, and how it is always the better road. This is why, besides the life and teaching of Jesus, one of the most important books of the New Testament to teach regularly is the book of James. It's the primer on how to live differently as a spiritual person.

And as I explain the gospel, the most important tightrope I walk is explaining the grace-truth dynamic within the gospel itself. This is so important to get right. Not only is it the heart of the gospel, but it is also at the heart of many of the most regrettable caricatures and stereotypes abounding about Christians and Christianity in our world today. At the most basic level, the goal is to hold both grace and truth together. Truth without grace is just judgment. Grace without truth is license. Only authentic Christianity brings together both truth and grace. Which isn't surprising, considering that this is precisely what Jesus brought when he came.

In John's Gospel, a theological bombshell was offered almost as an offhand comment: Jesus "came . . . full of grace and truth" (John 1:14). Jesus accepted the woman at the well despite her culturally scandalous ways, but he followed the acceptance by challenging her directly about her serial promiscuity. He stopped the stoning of a woman caught in adultery and made it clear he was not going to condemn her, but then he pointedly admonished her to turn from her adulterous ways. Grace *and* truth, as they flowed from Jesus, were inextricably intertwined. They also flowed from him in a way that was winsome. The very people he challenged about the state of their lives wanted him to come to their parties and meet their friends . . . and then challenge them! Jesus offered neither a feel-good theology that airbrushed out any real talk of sin nor legalistic attitudes of harsh condemnation and judgment. He came bringing grace and truth at their best and most compelling.

Most of us swing in one direction or another, either toward grace without truth or toward truth without grace. We either side with the woman caught in adultery and trumpet, "Neither do I condemn you," or we side with those who want to highlight "go and sin no more." Today, as previously discussed, I sense most are trending toward grace without truth. It's as if we are so ashamed of the judgmental, condemnatory nature of the church's recent history that we've swung as far in the other direction as we can. While understandable, the reality is that lukewarm religion holds little value in the midst of a settling secularism. What grips a conscience is anything *gripping*. If a worldview or faith lacks conviction, passion, or life change, then it is presenting itself as both privately and socially irrelevant. This means that the only kind of voice that will arrest the attention of the world will be convictional in nature, clear in its message, substantive in its content, and bold in its challenge. Translation: grace and truth in equal measure.

But explanation isn't the only rethinking at hand when it comes to evangelism. The second is to be quick about it.

Eight-Second Filters

What has been conventional wisdom is true: attention spans have been shrinking dramatically in recent years—more dramatically than most have realized. According to the research of the National Center for Biotechnology Information, the average attention span has dropped from 12 seconds in 2000 to just 8.25 seconds in 2015. That's around a 25 percent drop in just over a decade. To put that into perspective, the average attention span of a goldfish is 9 seconds. No, I did not make that up. We're .75 seconds less attentive than Bubbles. So what does 8.25 seconds of attention mean in day-in, day-out life? Here are some facts:

- percent of teens who forget major details of close friends and relatives: 25
- percent of people who forget their own birthdays from time to time: 7
- average number of times per hour an office worker checks their email inbox: 30[5]

So what does this mean for a church trying to reach out to an internet-based generation? Here are some internet browsing statistics that may cause you to rethink everything:

- average length watched of a single internet video: 2.7 minutes
- percent of page views that last less than 4 seconds: 17
- percent of page views that last more than 10 minutes: 4
- percent of words read on web pages with 111 words or less: 49
- percent of words read on an average (593 words) web page: 28[6]

Bottom line? Whatever it is we are attempting to convey, much less explain, will need to be communicated more frequently in shorter bursts of "snackable content." Why? Because members of Generation Z are the "ultimate consumers of snack media. They communicate in bite sizes."[7]

Some have suggested that what is really operating are highly evolved eight-second filters. Members of Generation Z, for example, are growing up in a world in which options and information are virtually limitless; time, of course, is not. So they have developed, almost out of necessity, the ability to quickly sort through enormous amounts of data. Or they rely on sources that do that for them, such as trending information within apps. The good news is that once something *does* gain their attention and is deemed worthy of time, they can become intensely committed and focused. The very internet that forced them to develop eight-second filters is the same internet that allows them to go deep on any topic they desire and to learn from a community of fellow interested parties. This means we can still engage people on a very deep level with truth. The bad news? We have eight seconds to get past their filters.[8] As one eighteen-year-old UCLA student said, "Generation Z takes in information instantaneously and loses interest just as fast."[9]

The *Wall Street Journal* chronicled how such insights are necessarily shaping every area of life, including sports. The St. Louis

Rams, for example, have one of the youngest teams in the NFL, with an average age of twenty-four. As coach Jeff Fisher put it, "Our players learn better with two phones and music going and with an iPad on the side. That's new."

So the Rams brought in a group of academics who run a research firm to evaluate their football teaching methods. They discovered that attention spans are shorter but that the players are savvier than ever because of their exposure to technology. So instead of having team meetings that last hours, followed by on-field practicing, "the team now has 10 to 15 minutes' worth of informational meetings and then hurries to the practice field to execute what they've just learned." Coaches also adjusted to the reality that most of their young players are visual learners who can best be reached by "a hundred different examples" of football scenarios. They also encourage their players to communicate with each other through apps such as Instagram and Snapchat.[10]

So rethinking evangelism involves (1) recapturing a sense of evangelism as both process and event, (2) having that process be heavily oriented toward explanation, and (3) having that explanation be conveyed in a quick and engaging manner in order to get past filters. That's why Dan Schawbel, managing partner of Millennial Branding, a New York consultancy, tells his advertising partners "that if they don't communicate in five words and a big picture, they will not reach this generation."[11] Which leads to an area that may need the most rethinking of all: that "big picture." In other words, the importance of being visual.

The Importance of the Visual

As I wrote in *The Rise of the Nones*, we have much we can learn from history about the importance of the visual.[12] The Lindisfarne Gospels is a thirteen-hundred-year-old manuscript revered to this day as the oldest surviving English version of the Gospels (see fig. 6.4).

Lindisfarne, often referred to as Holy Island, is a small island just off the Northumberland coast of England that is unreachable for several hours every day because of the tidal waters flowing around it.

A man named Eadfrith produced the Lindisfarne Gospels—a copy of the four Gospels of the New Testament—around AD 715 in honor of St. Cuthbert. Its pages reveal curvy, embellished letters, strange creatures, and spiraling symbols of exquisite precision and beauty. During the eighth century, spiritual pilgrims flocked to St. Cuthbert's shrine to see the Lindisfarne Gospels, making it one of the most visited and seen books of its day. The artwork and symbols on its pages helped convey the message of the Gospel to those who could not read.

Designed to be a visual, sensual, and artistic experience for its audience, the Lindisfarne Gospels is seen as a precursor to modern multimedia, according to Professor Richard Gameson from Durham University. "The emphasis," he says, "was to reach as many people as possible."[13] There are many strategies needed for the church to have an open "front door"—to help those who are unchurched to come and feel not only welcomed but also connected. What we can learn from the Lindisfarne Gospels is that in order to reach the culture today, the church needs to be visual—in our methods and in our explanations.

Over the last twenty years, the world has become increasingly visually based, with video and film becoming the most formative influences on culture. As mentioned, at the time the Lindisfarne Gospels was produced there was widespread illiteracy. People went on spiritual pilgrimages not only for the experience of seeing the relics and holy places they hoped would bestow grace but also to see the beautiful stained glass built into the cathedrals that told the story of faith in a medium they could understand: *pictures*.

It's no different today.

Generation Z is not only spiritually illiterate, but very visually oriented and informed. They consume knowledge of the world

Figure 6.4
Lindisfarne Gospels

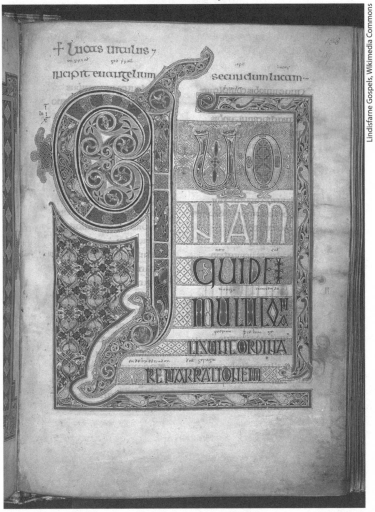

through YouTube, Netflix, Hulu—anything they find visually gripping. So when we plan the weekend services at Meck—which, for now, continues to remain our primary "front door" experience—there is very little we don't try to convey visually, whether during a song that is a part of worship or a point being made in the sermon. For example, before singing a song with the word "hallelujah" in it, we would show an introductory video explaining what the word means. We try to convey the "story" across multiple screens in multiple forms. It's simply how people best receive information and meaning, content and context.

But the need for the visual goes beyond something as basic as video. It's reflected in the changing nature of language itself.

The "Word" of the Year

The depth of this shift to the visual was evidenced when *Oxford Dictionary* named its 2015 word of the year. Here's the word:

Yes, it is a pictograph or, as it is more commonly called, an emoji. It is the "Face with Tears of Joy" emoji. While emojis have been around since the late 1990s, "2015 saw their use, and use of the word *emoji*, increase hugely." This particular emoji was selected because it was identified as the most used emoji globally in 2015.

In case you are a closet Luddite, an emoji is "a small digital image or icon used to express an idea or emotion in electronic communication." The term itself is Japanese in origin "and comes from *e* 'picture' + *moji* 'letter, character.' The similarity to the English word emoticon has helped its memorability and rise in use." An emoticon, by the way, is a "facial expression composed of keyboard characters, such as :), rather than a stylized image."[14]

The use of emojis reflects the cultural revolution that has come with technology in general and the smartphone in particular. It's also the only form of language that can transcend linguistic borders, serving the interconnected world of the internet, which knows no geopolitical or language boundaries. But more than anything, the use of emojis reflects the changing nature of communication itself. And when it comes to reaching the latest and largest generation—Generation Z—emojis are part of their language. The research of Sparks and Honey found that members of Generation Z "speak in emoticons and emojis. Symbols and glyphs provide context and create subtext so they can have private conversations. Emoji alphabets and icon 'stickers' replace text with pictures."[15] This is why, during a recent slate of Christmas Eve services, we presented the entire Christmas story through a video of two people texting each other using emojis, emoticons, and gifs. In other words, the way people today increasingly communicate. What follows is the script of the video.

Emoji Christmas Story

👦🎄🎁 Merry Christmas! 👧🎄🎁

You too! ❄️ ❄️ ❄️

I 😍🎄 !

I know! The 🎁 🎁 🎁 !

The 🍰🍪🍰🍪 !

👧 !

🎆 !!!

Wait . . . what's that?

A ⭐ ! You know 🌲 the Christmas story 🌲

😳 ????

You know 🙏☕😇

Right! 👩

Not really . . . 😬

Oh. 😐✋ I can tell you! 😃

👍👏

The full story is in the Bible 📖

Good to know 👍

So, the Virgin Mary . . . 👩 . . . was told by an 😇 that she was expecting a 👶 . . .

😱😮😱

And that 👶 = JESUS!!!

😮

And 👩 was like 😳

Ya think?! 😱

👰 and her fiancé Joseph 👱 got married 👰💍💎💐

And 👩 rode on a 🐴 to Bethlehem with her husband Joseph . . .

👍 I like the mustache 😄😂

There was no 🏠 to stay in tho for 👰👴 . . .

So they were forced to stay where all the animals were kept

Yeah it wasn't pretty.

What happened next?

Well there were 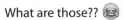 nearby . . .

What are those?? 😂

Shepherds! 😂 👍

Oh! 😆

An 😇 came to them and said:

"Fear not! I bring you great news and joy today. In the town of David a Savior has been born to you. He's the Messiah, the Lord. This will be a sign to you—you will find a baby wrapped in cloth and lying in a manger."

I bet the shepherds were like

Yep! They 🏃 to see 👶

There were also wise men 👳 💂 , who wished to 👀 a 👶 . . . So they followed a ⭐ that led to the 👶 . . . they brought
🎁 💝 🎁 🎈 🎉 🎊

123

🎉🎉 🎈🎈 HBD Jesus! 🎄

😃 It's awesome right?! And now we 🎉 on 🎄 to remember the 🎁 God gave us

And that 🎁 is . . . 👶 !!!!

👏👏👏 You got it!

See, I told my 👦 texting wasn't a waste of time!!

😂, I guess there's just 1 thing left to say . . . 🎼🎤 JOY TO THE WORLD!!!! 🎹🎷🎸👍

Invitation Works

About this time, you may be wondering how you will even get a chance to employ strategies like these with someone from Generation Z. It's not like they are lining up to have a chat with you.

But they could.

According to the research of the Barna Group, the unchurched continue to be most open to "a friend of yours inviting you to attend a local church," with one-fifth expressing strong interest and nearly half willing to consider a church based on this factor. "It's the top-rated way churches can establish connections with the unchurched."[16] With Generation Z, this approach can be especially effective, with 28 percent placing emphasis on their personal relationships compared to Millennials at 20 percent.[17] We've discussed eight-second attention spans for those in Generation Z. But when it comes to responding to a text or direct message from a friend? The Gen Z response is "immediate."[18] The personal and the relational cut through the noise of their lives.

The Great Enabler

But lest we think in too traditional of ways, we must realize that evangelism is not going to be something that takes place only in the context of a weekend service, much less within the context of a personal relationship. Evangelism's most common context may be online. Now don't think that means simply going online for Jesus. We must understand, first and foremost, how the internet is shaping the nature of choice and belief by becoming what I've called the "Great Enabler."

Through a search engine like Google, you can find not only a community in support of whatever choice you would like to make but also a clear apologetic for making it—and, if needed, the people and steps needed to pursue it. You want to pursue a gay lifestyle in a country like Pakistan where it is illegal? As one Pakistani told a reporter, "One of the first things I did online, maybe twelve years ago, was type in G-A-Y and hit search. Back then I found a group and made contact with twelve people in this city." The same article, focused on Google and sex, found a similar phenomenon in Britain with the growth of the fetish scene. Veteran "kinksters" in the UK tell how the internet completely transformed the number of people involved. Translation: it vastly increased those involved in the fetish scene.

As the article opines:

> Before the dawn of the Internet, people who experienced this urge would probably bury their desires deep down, maybe try to slake their needs with hard-to-obtain and dubious mail-order catalogues, or with sex phone lines.
>
> Now, they are only one click from a webpage that will explain—and crucially, normalize—those desires. There's usually an FAQ page, with "Am I crazy?" near the top. The answer, by the way, is always "No," and it's always society that's in the wrong. . . .
>
> The Internet also allows browsers to delve deeper, find online communities and forums, and reinforce their beliefs among a group

of people who, for the first time, won't challenge them or call them mad.

Sooner or later, whatever your bent, you can insulate yourself among like-minded people, until you think you're the normal one, and the rest of us are the intolerant.[19]

In a similar vein, the internet impacts faith. "Especially with young people . . . there's an openness with respect to choosing your religion, as opposed to just staying with the religion you're born into," says Christopher Smith, author of *Atheist Awakening*. "The Internet facilitates this: People who might otherwise feel isolated by the religious mores in their hometowns have access to communities of people who believe otherwise." This corresponds with the staggeringly high number of atheists who are, themselves, young. An estimated 42 percent of all atheists are between eighteen and twenty-nine years old.[20]

So evangelism will require not only fresh approaches to content but also new methods of communication. To stand on Mars Hill today will necessarily involve sitting behind a screen, entering into an insular world that many inhabit, all to attempt to offer a compelling alternative to the life they've been living. Members of Generation Z are "agile communicators: speed of communication and repartee garners cultural currency," note Sparks and Honey. "They're accustomed to rapid-fire banter and commentary."[21]

Give it to them.

Engage their questions, their viewpoints, and their perspectives. Enter into their chat rooms, respond to their blogs, answer their tweets. The news is filled with the success of ISIS in luring young people to their radicalized version of Islam through the internet. As the *New York Times* has detailed, "The reach of the Islamic State's recruiting effort has been multiplied by an enormous cadre of operators on social media. The terrorist group itself maintains a 24-hour online operation, and its effectiveness is vastly extended by larger rings of sympathetic volunteers and fans who pass on its messages and viewpoint, reeling in potential recruits."[22]

Christian evangelists need to take a page from the very same playbook, because it's the playbook for an entire generation.

A Theology of Evangelism

But we can't make evangelism simply about tactics. The heart of the problem with evangelizing any generation in a post-Christian world is Christians who don't feel they need evangelizing. Buried within Pew's study on the American religious landscape was a startling find. Adults who identify with a specific religion were asked whether they see their religion as "the one, true faith leading to eternal life" or if, in their view, "many religions can lead to eternal life." How we answer such a question will determine whether evangelism is integral or peripheral, a matter of urgency or complacency.

In a stunning revelation, among Christians, two-thirds said many religions can lead to eternal life, and most of them (50 percent of all Christians) said some non-Christian religions can lead to life everlasting.[23] With such a mindset in play, we should not be surprised at tepid attempts at evangelism. And when attempted, poor results.

Recently, the Church of England went so far as to signal to its members that it does more harm than good for them to speak openly about their faith when it comes to spreading Christianity. Internal research found that "practicing Christians who talk to friends and colleagues about their beliefs are three times as likely to put them off God as to attract them." Solution? Let's stop talking to them. This response despite the fact that the same survey found that four out of ten British adults did not even think Jesus was a "real person who actually lived." Among those under the age of thirty-five, one out of every four believed him to be a fictional character.[24]

So perhaps the key is learning how to talk about Jesus in a good way. An effective way. A bridge-building way. Which is, of course, the purpose and role of apologetics.

Discussion Questions

1. What does it mean to see evangelism as both process and event? How does that differ from past approaches?
2. If you're being honest, does your outreach strategy reflect an Acts 2 or an Acts 17 approach? Why do you say that?
3. What does it mean for our primary cultural currency in the church to be explanation when it comes to evangelism? How are you currently involving explanation in your evangelism strategy? How might you begin to do so?
4. Sometimes in the church we're so used to talking to the already convinced that we lose a sense of what it means to talk to someone who isn't. Based on what you've read so far, have you lost touch with the mindset of the average person today? Reflect on that, however painful it may be.
5. What makes the grace and truth balance so hard? How can your church improve the balance in your ministry?
6. Should your ministry change in light of the fact that people today have an average attention span of just over eight seconds? If so, how? If not, why not?
7. With the shaping of worldviews that happens so effectively through visual media, are there ways you can begin leveraging video, images, or other visual media to better translate the gospel to your audience?

7

Apologetics
for a New Generation

You know that each evangelist
Who tells the passion of Lord Jesus Christ
Says not in all things as his fellows do,
. . . For some of them say more and some say less
When they His piteous passion would express.

Geoffrey Chaucer

Recently, I was interviewed for a National Public Radio program. The host and I had a good conversation about faith and culture, and we continued talking after the program. When he got me alone and off the air, he said, "Can I ask you a question? You're a Christian, and you seem intelligent, so answer me this: What the duck is up with this idea that the earth is only six or seven thousand years old?"

Only he didn't say "duck."

It just rhymed with "duck."

Let's not get into young earth versus old earth. Here's what everyone *should* get into: the "What is up with" questions. Why? Because they are the heart of what is churning around in the minds of those on the outside looking in at the Christian faith. These people have so many of these types of questions, and the essence of any conversation that might move them down the spiritual road will involve talking about them.

And without defensiveness.

It's simply a cultural reality that people in a post-Christian world are genuinely incredulous that anyone would think like . . . well, a Christian—or at least, what it means in their minds to think like a Christian. So of course they are going to ask:

"What is up with not wanting two people who love each other to get married?"

"What is up with thinking sex is so bad?"

"What is up with a loving God sending someone like Gandhi to hell?"

I'm sure you can think of any number of questions.

Answering the "What is up with" questions is what lies at the heart of modern-day apologetics, the pre-evangelism so missing in churches. Apologetics also involves defending the character of God. Many look at the workings of the world and feel like they would act more justly than God appears to be acting. It also involves addressing the most pressing barriers post-Christians have to all things religious, which often have less to do with intellectual issues than emotional ones. As noted earlier, when those outside the faith look at those inside the faith, they don't think we look very much like our Leader. So apologetics must grapple with the great indictments the world lays at the feet of the church, such as judgmentalism, hypocrisy, anti-intellectualism, a perceived lack of tolerance, and legalism.

That's why at Meck we do series that actually address these very issues in as direct a way as possible. For example, a series titled "Judged" looked at how judgmentalism works in our world. Or the series "In Search of a Better God" examined how we put God in the dock for our perceived sense of his injustice. The goal is to continually uphold and defend, explain and examine the character of God.

Spiritually Illiterate

But apologetics for Generation Z runs deeper than answering new questions or addressing new barriers. Apologetics, in many ways, is at its best when it finds the cultural bridges we can walk across, and then, while walking, address the questions and barriers that exist along that path. With that in mind, what are the most powerful, fruitful bridges to cross?

Perhaps the most defining mark of members of Generation Z, in terms of their spiritual lives, is their spiritual illiteracy. This is, of course, the defining mark of the post-Christian world. They do not know what the Bible says. They do not know the basics of Christian belief or theology. They do not know what the cross is about. They do not know what it means to worship. But their spiritual illiteracy is deeper than that. They are more than post-Christian. They don't even have a memory of the gospel.

As a result, there is a profound spiritual emptiness. They've never encountered God, experienced God. They are left feeling the sickness of the world's disease without a narrative, without a story, without a transcendent meaning or purpose. They have a crisis in values; they find themselves needing them but not having them and divorced from any means of finding them. They have a lack of vision; nothing is calling them upward to be more than they are beyond themselves. Yet they cannot help but be incurably spiritual. That is the defining mark of what it means to be human. We are made in the image of God, which means we have been created to be able to respond to and be in a relationship with the living God.

So how is the vacuum being filled?

Largely through the occult and, ironically, science. Not exactly dancing partners. Yet these are the bridges over which we must learn to walk, addressing the key questions and barriers facing a faith narrative. Let's begin with the occult.

Ghosts Skew Better

Like many Europeans, Marianne Haaland Bogdanoff, a travel agency manager in Norway, does not go to church, except maybe at Christmas, and is doubtful about the existence of God. But she believes in ghosts, even calling in a clairvoyant to solve some troubling supernatural occurrences that were happening in her office.

She's not alone.

While Norwegian churches may be empty and belief in God in sharp decline, "belief in, or at least fascination with, ghosts and spirits is surging. Even Norway's royal family, which is required by law to belong to the Evangelical Lutheran Church, has flirted with ghosts, with a princess coaching people on how to reach out to spirits." Roar Fotland, a Methodist preacher and assistant professor at the Norwegian School of Theology in Oslo, notes that "God is out but spirits and ghosts are filling the vacuum." It's an important dynamic to understand.[1]

Pitirim Sorokin, the founder of Harvard University's department of sociology, argued that the pendulum of civilization generally swings in one of two directions: the ideational and the sensate. The ideational civilization is more theological and spiritual, while the sensate culture is more rational or scientific. Sorokin contended that the classic ideational period was the medieval. From the Enlightenment forward, we lived in a sensate world. Sorokin's thesis rings true. Now in our struggle with what the modern world has given to us—or, more accurately, taken away—there seems to be a swing back toward the ideational.[2]

We live in a world that is more open than ever to spiritual things. Not defined religion, mind you, but spirituality. And specifically, the supernatural. A keenly felt emptiness, resulting from a secularized, materialistic world, has led to a hunger for something more, but many are unable to go further than the search for an *experience*. As a result, an extraterrestrial will serve as well as an angel, a spiritualist as well as a minister. Borrowing from the late historian Christopher Dawson, we have a new form of secularism that offers "religious emotion divorced from religious belief."[3]

So God is out, but ghosts are in.

This situation reminds me of something CBS head Leslie Moonves once said when unveiling a fall television lineup heavy on the occult in order to reach a younger demographic in a state of cultural change. After canceling Emmy-nominated and critically acclaimed *Joan of Arcadia*, in which a young woman speaks to God, in favor of *The Ghost Whisperer*, a supernatural drama about a woman who communicates with the spirit world, Moonves declared, "I think talking to ghosts may skew younger than talking to God."[4]

He was right. Even as I write, a new challenge game is going viral. It's about connecting with a dead spirit from Mexico named Charlie. Fueled by thousands of videos from young people supposedly showing "contact," the game is played by placing two pencils in the shape of a cross on a piece of paper with the words *yes* and *no*. Those present then repeat the phrase, "Charlie, Charlie can we play?" in order to make contact with the demon. If Charlie is there, the pencils are said to move toward his answer. If he is present, then questions of any kind are asked . . . and answered. To end the game, players say, "Charlie, Charlie can we stop?"

The word *occult* means that which is hidden or secret beyond the range of ordinary human knowledge or below the surface of normal life. When used in that sense, it's almost a neutral term. But it has come to be used as a reference to those practices that link up, intentionally or not, with the hidden, or secret, world of Satan and his demons. And that is not neutral. Then the occult involves engaging the forces of darkness, connecting with Satan and his fellow demons. When people do that, they willfully open the doors of their lives to Satan's presence and activity.

What are the marks of the occult?

The first characteristic is the disclosure or communication of information unavailable to humans through normal means. This involves things such as horoscopes, fortune-telling, psychic hot-lines, and tarot cards.

The second mark of things occultic has to do with the placing of persons in contact with supernatural powers, paranormal energies, or demonic forces. This mark entails an attempt to summon up a spirit or a deceased relative through a séance, channeling a spirit, or procuring the services of someone claiming to be a medium.

The third mark of the world of the occult is any attempt to gain and master power in order to manipulate or influence other people into certain actions. This mark includes all forms of witchcraft and the casting of spells.

There is no dead spirit from Mexico named Charlie. There are, however, demons only too happy for the ruse. And the open door.[5]

There is one aspect of this turn to the supernatural that works in our favor—namely, that Christianity is very much a faith in the supernatural. We can speak to all things in the spirit world with clarity and definition as well as caution and warning. I know that at Meck some of our most popular and apologetically fruitful series have been on the paranormal world, mapping out the supernatural world biblically and reviewing the marks of the occult.

But there is another aspect of this interest in the supernatural that can help us reach a post-Christian world. Whenever I speak on the missional challenge of our day, particularly overseas, I am often asked where "signs and wonders" fit into things. The more I've re-flected on this topic, the more I believe it may fit quite strategically.

Too many Christians have stripped their faith of its supernatural elements, whittling the spiritual dynamic down to quiet times and promptings. Theologically, we believe in miracles and healings and pray for them regularly. Functionally, not so much. Yet biblically, the primary role of a miracle (or sign, or wonder) is to authenticate biblical revelation in fresh missional settings.

To be sure, miracles and miraculous signs and wonders are just that—miraculous. They are out of the ordinary; they are not commonplace. Otherwise they would cease to be miraculous. They are extraordinary events, creative deviations from God's normal and natural ways of working—that's the very definition of a miracle, a sign, or a wonder. Even within the ministry of Christ, peppered as it was with miracles, they proved to be a very small part of his day-in, day-out ministry. In fact, huge portions of the Bible go without miracles altogether, and significant men and women of God whose lives are recorded in the Bible, such as John the Baptist (John 10:41), experienced no miracles whatsoever.

Yet the purpose and function of miracles were clear. Miracles and miraculous signs and wonders are found in four main clusters in the Bible. First, they cluster around Moses (e.g., plagues of Egypt, crossing the Red Sea, manna from heaven). Second, they cluster around the prophets, such as Elijah and Elisha. Third, they cluster around Jesus himself. And fourth, they cluster around the apostles. Miracles in the Bible by and large cluster around these four poles, which represent the four main epochs of revelation— the four main eras when God was breaking out, making himself known, and releasing the Bible's message. Through Moses, God brought the law. Through the prophets, he delivered the prophetic word. Through Jesus, he revealed his teaching and the very gospel itself. Through the apostles, he gave the New Testament writings.

It would seem clear that the major purpose of miracles was to authenticate each fresh stage of God's revelation, drawing our attention to what God wanted us to take note of, revealing that it really was from him. Moses was a prime example: "How will they believe me?" he asked. God's answer? He would perform signs and wonders.

Fast-forward to Acts 2:22, where Peter says that the ministry of Jesus was accredited by signs and wonders and miracles (the same is said in Heb. 2:3–4). And throughout the book of Acts, the miracles were done not just by anyone but by and large through the apostles—the only two exceptions were by men who were specifically commissioned by the apostles. And Paul, in 2 Corinthians 12:12, points out that what marks an apostle are signs, wonders, and miracles—in order to authenticate their position and message.

From this, it shouldn't surprise a Christian that missionaries going to previously unreached people groups experience the advent of signs and wonders through their ministries at an uncommon rate. The reason would seem to be that such miracles are simply fulfilling their intent—authenticating the fresh outbreak of God's Word. Might not the case be the same in cultures that are increasingly post-Christian yet wildly interested in the supernatural? All I know is that in many pockets of the Western world that are the most advanced in their post-Christian status, people are finding that signs and wonders, in their proper biblical place, penetrate deeply secular minds.[6]

But there is another, equally strategic bridge we can cross. We can speak to people's interest in the awe and wonder of the universe.

The Heavens Declare

Within our world, there is an amazingly deep sense of awe and wonder about the universe. And the ones who feel this the most? Younger Millennials, also known as Generation Z. As figure 7.1 indicates, nearly half (49 percent) express this feeling, up dramatically from earlier studies.[7]

This openness to spirituality via cosmology was confirmed in another research project, conducted by LifeWay (see fig. 7.2), which found that "more than 4 in 10 of the nonreligious believe physics and humanity point to a creator." Further, they are more likely to agree than disagree with the statement, "Since the universe has organization, I think there is a creator who designed it." Granted, younger Americans are more likely than older Americans to believe human life may exist without a Creator, but with 72 percent of

Figure 7.1

Growing Shares Experience Regular Feelings of Spiritual Peace, Well-Being, and Wonder about Universe

Percent of US adults who feel . . . at least once a week
. . . a deep sense of spiritual peace and well-being

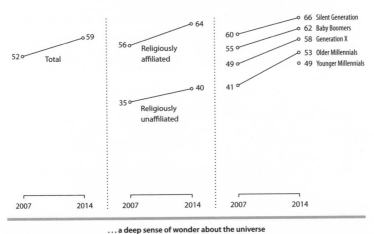

. . . a deep sense of wonder about the universe

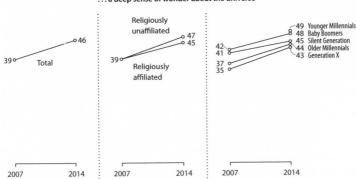

Source: 2014 Religious Landscape Study, conducted June 4–September 30, 2014, Pew Research Center.

all Americans who agree that human life is evidence of a Creator, we have fertile ground. As LifeWay's research director concluded, "Traditional evidences for belief in a creator resonate with most Americans."[8]

I have found that discussing the awe and wonder of the universe, openly raising the many questions surrounding the universe and then positing the existence of God, is one of the most valuable

Figure 7.2

Is There a Creator?

Comparing Views of Nonreligious and All Americans

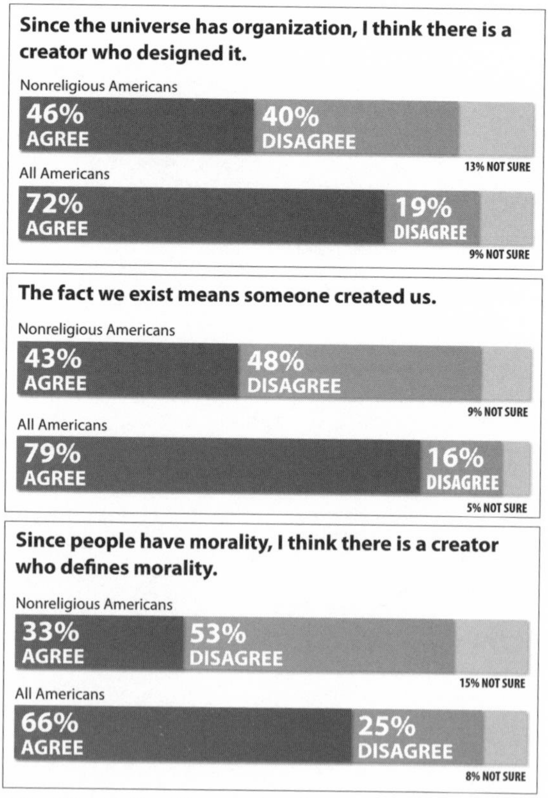

Since the universe has organization, I think there is a creator who designed it.

Nonreligious Americans

46% AGREE   40% DISAGREE   13% NOT SURE

All Americans

72% AGREE   19% DISAGREE   9% NOT SURE

The fact we exist means someone created us.

Nonreligious Americans

43% AGREE   48% DISAGREE   9% NOT SURE

All Americans

79% AGREE   16% DISAGREE   5% NOT SURE

Since people have morality, I think there is a creator who defines morality.

Nonreligious Americans

33% AGREE   53% DISAGREE   15% NOT SURE

All Americans

66% AGREE   25% DISAGREE   8% NOT SURE

Source: LifeWay, http://www.lifewayresearch.com/2015/10/07/nonreligious-americans
-see-evidence-of-creator/.

Note: Totals may not equal 100% due to rounding.

apologetics/pre-evangelism approaches that can be pursued. The existence of human life, the complexity of the universe, and even the starting point of a Big Bang resonate deeply with nonbelievers and provide numerous opportunities to present a coherent and compelling case for God.

So what would that kind of an apologetic approach feel and sound like? Let's use the Big Bang as an example.

The Big Bang

Recently, a discovery was made that few scientists thought would ever be discovered at all, much less in their lifetimes: ripples made in the fabric of the universe following the Big Bang. Scientists believed that gravitational waves, first predicted by Einstein, were common, constantly crashing over the earth, but they had never been able to detect them.

Then they did.

The ripples confirmed a theory that had been tantalizing scientists for decades—namely, that the Big Bang wasn't just big; it was fast. As in almost instantaneously, miraculously fast—beyond even the speed of light (which was previously thought to have been impossible). In fact, it happened when the universe was only a trillionth of a trillionth of a trillionth of a second old. As first posited by MIT physicist Alan Guth, the event is called inflation and refers to the universe going from something smaller than the end of your little finger to one hundred trillion trillion times that size.

The idea of the Big Bang was first put forward by Edwin Hubble, for whom the Hubble Space Telescope was named. His theory was that at one time all matter was packed into a dense mass at temperatures of many trillions of degrees. Then about 13.8 billion years ago, there was a huge explosion. And from that explosion, all of the matter that today forms our planets and stars was born. Hubble's idea was confirmed through what had been called the discovery of the century. On April 24, 1992, the Cosmic Background Explorer satellite, better known as COBE, gave stunning confirmation of the hot Big Bang creation event.

But how did the expansion following the Big Bang take place? If it was a bang that expanded, how did it spread out so far with such equal temperatures? Now we know. As *USA Today*'s coverage reported, "It underwent a fast and incomprehensibly massive growth spurt in its earliest infancy."[9] In other words, as we might say, it was a start of biblical proportions. Miraculous, even. Who, or what, can go beyond the speed of light and spread out the entire universe instantly from a single explosion? Sounds like an "in the beginning God created" moment.

We already knew the Big Bang pointed to something outside our boundaries of knowledge. It doesn't take a physicist to wonder what made the Big Bang bang and even less of one to ask, "If nothing existed before the Big Bang, then where did the stuff that got banged come from?" As Alan Guth himself once noted, even if you could come up with a theory that would account for the creation of something from nothing through the laws of physics, you'd still have to account for the origin of the laws of physics.[10]

Do you see how ripe this is for spiritual conversations directly addressing the awe and wonder people already feel when contemplating the universe? As the apostle Paul wrote in Romans, "For since the creation of the world God's invisible qualities—his eternal power and divine nature—have been clearly seen, being understood from what has been made" (1:20). Even those in science itself are starting to play along in a way that those trying to reach a post-Christian generation should closely follow.

A Post-Empirical God

The famed scientist Ian Barbour once observed that when religion first met modern science in the seventeenth century, the encounter was a friendly one. "By the eighteenth century many scientists believe in a God who had designed the universe, but they no longer believe in a personal God actively involved in the world and human life. By the nineteenth century," Barbour concluded, "scientists were hostile to religion."[11] And the crux of that hostility is rooted in what can be called a reductive naturalism. Naturalism is the idea that nature is "all that is." Reductive naturalism posits that all that can be known within nature is that which can be *empirically verified*.

So a reductive naturalism contends that what is real is only that which can be seen, tasted, heard, smelled, or touched, then *verified*, meaning able to be replicated in a test tube. Knowledge is "reduced" to this level of knowing. If something cannot be examined in a tangible, scientific manner, it is not simply unknowable; it is meaningless. This naturalism holds that life is accidental. There is nothing beyond ourselves that will ever bring order, reason, or explanation. We must restrict what can be known to what is immediately before us, to what is "given" or "factual." This means (again) what can be empirically, or scientifically, demonstrated.

As astronomer Carl Sagan argued in his final work, the goal is to rid ourselves of a "demon-haunted" world, meaning anything that would challenge the rule of science and technology as the ultimate arbiter of truth and reality, for there is no other truth or reality to embrace.[12]

So much for God. At least, that was then.

But this is now.

There is now a battle raging over the scientific method itself, particularly between those engaged in cosmology and those pursuing the study of fundamental physics. Quick primer: cosmology is the study of the universe as a whole (e.g., the Big Bang). Fundamental physics is the study of reality's bedrock entities and their interactions (e.g., the interaction of matter, energy, space, and time).

Here's the battle. Some scientists want to argue that if a theory is coherent, it does not need to be tested experimentally to be valid.

In other words, scientific knowledge does not need to be empirical. The reason some are arguing for this reformulation is because such things as string theory and the idea of a multiverse turn old understandings of what constitutes physical reality on their head.

(Don't worry if you don't know what either of these ideas entails—hang with the big picture of empiricism for a moment.)

These new theories are raising questions about the very rules of science when applied to the universe as a whole, because both string theory and a multiverse posit entities that may very well be unobservable or beyond our "horizon." In other words, while they may be true, their very nature means they can never be subject to empirical verification. This is being called post-empirical science. As a result, philosophers of physics such as Richard Dawid are arguing that in spite of the fact that there is no "evidence" for string theory, it still should be considered the most likely candidate for future research and consideration. As Dawid contends, "No one has found a good alternative to string theory."

Going further, Sean Carroll—a highly respected and philosophically astute physicist—notes that "whether or not we can observe [extra dimensions or other universes] directly, the entities involved in these theories are either real or they are not. Refusing to contemplate their possible existence on the grounds of some *a priori* principle, even though they might play a crucial role in how the world works, is as non-scientific as it gets." As an NPR report on the matter concluded, "Even if a theory predicts entities that can't be directly observed, if there are indirect consequences of their existence we can confirm, then those theories (and those entities) must be included in our considerations."[13]

Precisely.

And this was the prime argument brought by theists against the Enlightenment, which sought to bracket off any consideration of God. If God could not be seen, tasted, touched, heard, or smelled, he was deemed irrelevant to scientific inquiry, much less scientific verification. The next logical step? God was obviously nonexistent. Sweet irony that it is science itself that is bringing the consideration of God back into play—and making him intellectually sound.

In many ways, it is the blending of the supernatural and science that provides the apologetic opening to Generation Z. They believe in the supernatural—nothing stirs them more than the cosmos in terms of awe and wonder—which makes them open to supernatural explanations of the universe.

I am reminded of those wonderful words penned by Robert Jastrow, who for twenty years was the director of NASA's Goddard Institute for Space Studies, as he reflected on the pursuit of ultimate truth: "For the scientist who has lived by his faith in the power of reason, the story ends like a bad dream. He has scaled the mountains of ignorance; he is about to conquer the highest peak; as he pulls himself over the final rock, he is greeted by a band of theologians who have been sitting there for centuries."[14] No wonder that post-empirical science is being called science's most dangerous idea.

It may just lead to God. And lead others to him as well.

I was walking out of a grocery store recently when I heard someone calling, "Pastor White! Pastor White!" I turned around and saw a young man walking up to me. "I just wanted to introduce myself," he said. "Your church has changed my life."

He was a sophomore in college, and his girlfriend had invited him to Meck. He told me he came as an atheist but then became a Christian, had been baptized at our last baptism event, and just the month before had attended our membership class and become a member of the church.

"I just wanted to thank you," he said.

I gave him a big hug, and by this time, his girlfriend had joined us. She got a hug too.

They turned to leave, and then he came back and said, "One other thing. I think scientifically, and the way you talked about science, that's what got me. That's where I had the most questions. That's where you gave me the answers I needed."

Discussion Questions

1. Imagine yourself in the author's shoes when asked by the radio host, "What the [bleep] is up with this idea that the earth is only six or seven thousand years old?" Without focusing on the particular topic of the question, how would you respond? Does even imagining that scenario make you nervous? What might that mean for your approach to apologetics?

2. We live in a world that is more open than ever to spiritual things. Not defined religion, but spirituality in general. How do you see this manifested in the world? What might that mean for the church and its mission to reach people?

3. In our world today, there is a deep sense of awe and wonder, particularly among Generation Z. How might your church incorporate or inspire a sense of awe and wonder about the universe?

4. When you read through the apologetic regarding the Big Bang, what was your reaction? Why do you think you felt that way?

5. How is science bringing the consideration of God back into play in the modern mind?

6. How does the blending of science and spirituality help provide an apologetic opening to Generation Z?

8

Decisions

Life is short, and Art long; the crisis fleeting; experience perilous, and decision difficult.

Hippocrates

A characterless man never reaches a decision.

Georg Wilhelm Friedrich Hegel

As we come to the end of our journey, it is a time for decisions. At Mecklenburg Community Church, we've made eight strategic decisions in light of everything you've read that we are convinced have enabled us to be effective at reaching not only the unchurched but also the unchurched nones and, even at this early stage, Generation Z. Two have already been detailed: we have made the decisions to rethink evangelism and to do so in light of an Acts 17 model, in essence, chapters 4 through 7. Following are six others we consider just as decisive.

Be Cultural Missionaries

We have become cultural missionaries and act according to that identity. I think we all know what a good missionary would do if dropped into the darkest recesses of the Amazon basin to reach an unreached people group. They would learn the language, try to understand the customs and rituals, and work to translate the Scriptures, particularly the message of the gospel, into the indigenous language. When it comes to worship, they would incorporate the musical styles and instruments of the people. They might even attempt to dress more like them. In short, they would try to build every cultural bridge they could into the world of that unreached people group in order to bring Christ to bear.

Why is it that what would be so natural, so obvious, so clear to do in that missiological setting is so resisted in the West?

In being cultural missionaries, we have also decided to be laser sharp in our focus. Much has been written, for example, about disaffected Christian Millennials who are leaving the church. In fact, there seemed to be a season when the evangelical publishing world was fixated on why Christian Millennials were leaving the church. So the evangelical subculture got them to write blogs, articles, and books about their disaffection and from this extrapolated what the church has to do and where it has to change in order to reach that generation for Christ.

Frankly, we're not that interested. Our mission is not the already convinced. Why focus on *Christian* Millennials who leave the church in order to learn how to reach *non*-Christian Millennials who are *not* in the church? That's misplaced missional energy. Disaffected Christian Millennials are not abandoning Christ, just the church. Okay, so did their parents. And their parents before them. They either came back to the church or reinvented it stylistically.

Not exactly news.

What *is* news is the rise of the nones, those Millennials (and every other generation) who are abandoning religion altogether.

Not to mention the coming juggernaut of Generation Z and their post-Christian minds. So the real story you need to get as a leader isn't about Christians wanting more of a narrative, wishing their pastor was more like Donald Miller, hating the big-stage production of the eighties megachurch, or anything else of that nature. That's an evangelical subculture thing. The real issue is much larger. So if we are going to talk to someone and listen to someone and learn from someone, let's talk, listen, and learn from those who have not been Christians, much less churched. After all, they are the true mission field.

Skew Young

One of the natural flows of the church, which I first wrote about in my book *What They Didn't Teach You in Seminary*, is that left to itself the church will grow old.[1] It *will* age. First you'll lose the twentysomethings, then the thirtysomethings, and on the creep will go. And that means, by default, you will not reach the coming generations. While the goal is not to simply be a church for young people (I've often blogged about the importance of having older members willing to invest in leadership, in service, and in mentoring the next generation), neither is the goal to be a church for old people—a church that will have one generational cycle before closing its doors.

If the natural flow of the church is to skew older, the leadership of the church must invest a disproportionate amount of energy and intentionality in order to maintain a vibrant population of young adults. At Meck we have used three simple strategies not only to maintain influence on the culture of our day but also to impact the next generation.

First, to attract young people, you have to hire young people. I know that for many people in senior leadership, the thought of having a staff filled with twentysomethings can be intimidating.

At Meck, nearly half of our staff are in their twenties and we love it—the young and the old. The younger staff bring fresh insight and perspective on reaching and connecting with the younger generations. When asking one staff member what they valued about working at Meck, this was their response: "For me, working here is fun because it's challenging. . . . We're constantly challenged to move to the next level, the next step, the next vision. . . . All the while we are asked to keep in mind that we're not chasing the next fad but rather the next God-ordained project to get more unchurched people in our doors."

Second, who you platform is who you attract. From the people on stage in the band to the greeters standing at the doors, it is important to platform those who are young because people are drawn to others who are like them.

Third, to attract young people, you have to acknowledge young people. While every aspect of the service does not need to be designed just for them, and the church cannot "cater" specifically to young people, those who are younger do need to be acknowledged. What does this mean? It means that you take into account their world and all that includes: tastes, priorities, questions, vocabulary, sensibilities, and most definitely their technology. The church needs to learn to embrace the technology of the next generation, as it will fast become the technology for us all. Bottom line? Sometimes bridging a cultural divide is as simple as who you hire, who you put on stage, and who you acknowledge.

Target Men

Another strategic decision we have made is to unashamedly target men in our outreach, in our messages, in our . . . well, almost everything. We have become convinced through years of experience that if you get the man, you get everyone else within his orbit—specifically, his wife and his children. We have not found the same to be true by targeting women. In fact, churches filled with Christian "widows" (women in attendance while their husbands stay home) is almost proverbial. Truth be told, most churches are oriented toward women. The messages, ministries, outreach, décor, music, videos—they're all designed for women.

What does it mean to target men? It means you think about male sensibilities in terms of music and message, vocabulary and style. For example, have you noticed how much contemporary worship feels like it's saying, "Jesus is my boyfriend" when you listen to the lyrics? What guy wants to sing that? No guy I know. So we don't sing those songs. When I give a message, I talk like a man talks, specifically, the way a man talks with other men. Direct and maybe a little rough around the edges. But men talk football, not fashion. So I cater to a man's humor, his interests, his world, his way of thinking, his questions. And I deliver those talks the way I would talk to a guy. When it comes to crafting an invitational outreach tool—such as a gift to be given out to invite someone to a Christmas Eve service—we don't fill it with recipes but with a hefty mug.

One of the most frequent things we hear from women is, "My husband loves this church. I could never get him to church before. But now he comes here even when I don't!" And she will go where he wants to go. Get him, you get her. Get him and her, you get the family.

It's as simple as that.

Prioritize Children's Ministry

Quick—what is the most important outreach ministry in the life of your church? If you hesitated for even one second before answering "children's ministry," then you need to read everything I am going to say next with the greatest of attention.

At Meck, we prioritize children's ministry above every other ministry. Why? Because it is the most important ministry for the mission of the church. Let me tell you a story that may help answer why.

When our kids were young, my family and I went to a church while on our summer study break. It was a new church, very small, that was meeting in a movie theater. How can I say this? . . . It was one of the most programming-challenged services I've ever attended. It was so bad that we were looking at our watches *five minutes* after the service started. When the service mercifully ended, we wanted to get out of there and never return. I know, that isn't very gracious, and I should have been more focused on worshiping Jesus, but you would have wanted to leave too.

But when we went to pick up our kids, they were having an absolute blast. They didn't want to leave! A couple had poured themselves into that ministry and made it really, really good. I still recall how they had transformed a meager space into a time machine with special-effects music that took the kids "back" into Bible times. New kids, such as ours, were treated extraspecial and taken to a treasure chest full of small toys from which they could choose, just for coming the first time. The amount of money this took? Next to nothing. The money spent on state-of-the-art facilities? It was a theater rented by a church plant. The time and intentionality? Now that was priceless.

We went to some of the "best" churches in the area that summer, but our kids *pleaded* with us to take them back to the one we could barely stand. Now, if I lived there and felt compelled to find a church home as a father of four, do you think I would have at least given that church another try? You can count on it. Most parents would. Here's the lesson: you can drop the ball in the service but ace it with the kids and still have a chance that a family will return. But no matter how good the service is, if the children's ministry is bad, the family won't come back.

Too many people treat children's ministry as a necessary evil. It's often severely underfunded, understaffed, and underappreciated.

Wake up. Children are the heart of your growth engine. If a none ever were to come to your church uninvited, it would probably be for the sake of their kids. If a none comes because they were invited, what you do with their children will be a deal breaker. And if you want to reach Generation Z? Many of them are in your children's ministry right now or will be reached only if they choose to enter it. Make sure that when they do, it is an experience that will have them begging to come back.

Cultivate a Culture of Invitation

As mentioned earlier, in Michael Green's seminal work on the staggering growth of the early church, he had one huge conclusion: they shared the good news of Jesus like gossip over the backyard fence. In other words, a culture of invitation was both cultivated and celebrated. At Meck, that's what we do and what we're after.

It's not difficult.

We talk about inviting our friends and family all the time.

We create tools to put in the hands of people to use to invite their friends all the time.

We celebrate and honor people who invite people all the time.

Such tools can be something as simple as pens with the name of our church and our website on them that people can give to someone, whether a friend they run into in the grocery store or a waiter at a restaurant. During the summer, we might hand out empty pizza boxes with a card inside inviting them to Meck and a voucher for a free pizza—no strings attached. For special times in the life of the church, like Easter and Christmas, we design tools to be fun—fun to give and fun to receive. People use these tools all the time to reach out to their unchurched family, friends, neighbors, and anyone else they interact with in their orbit.

Disciple Your Mission

For all of you wondering about discipleship, here's your moment. We take discipleship as seriously as anyone—maybe more. We've simply determined that there is a need for a third leg on the stool.

Let me explain.

Most churches have two legs on their stool. One is the weekend with all of its services and events, and the other is small groups. There's a third, strategic leg that is entirely missing. We feel there needs to be a third leg that is completely devoted to discipleship. Yes, I know, many churches feel that both weekend services and small groups should be discipleship oriented. We disagree. The weekend service should be, at least for now, the front door of the church for outreach. As a result, it should be crafted optimally for that outreach. That often means it is not crafted optimally for discipleship.

Every church must also decide if small groups are for outreach, discipleship, or care and assimilation. We have never felt they are best for outreach or ideal for discipleship. We chose to have our small groups for care and assimilation. And the entry points for our small groups are designed for people who have never thought of them, much less been in one before. So we gather groups of 150 to 200 for a meal, organize them into small groups (based on life stage, where they live, etc), and invite them to continue gathering together once a week for six weeks. After that time, they have the option to continue meeting together as a small group.

So where does discipleship find its home?

The third leg.

We created the Meck Institute, a community-college approach to discipleship that offers classes, seminars, experiences, and events designed wholly for spiritual growth and formation. Like classes at a community college, new classes and experiences launch each season: spring, summer, fall, and winter. They are offered on all days of the week at a variety of times, and we also have online classes. Offerings include the most foundational of all classes—titled "Foundations," I might add, addressing how to be sure you are a Christian, how to pray, how to read the Bible, and how to have a quiet time—all the way to seminary-level courses on systematic theology.

I cannot begin to express how important it is to "disciple your mission." I've never heard that phrase, so let me coin it. To "disciple your mission" means that you develop your discipleship, first and foremost, around who it is you are trying to reach. We are trying to reach the unchurched and, even more than that, the nones, in view of the pressing challenge of the rise of Generation Z. So our discipleship is going to be twofold: serve the needs of our existing believers for missional engagement and disciple the newly converted on the most foundational aspects of Christian life and thought.

What, you might ask, of the needs of existing believers who want to be fed? If you mean titillated by the latest biblical insights slathered on an already calorie-rich meal they have been feasting on for the last several years, we honestly don't care.

The Secret Sauce

But here's the secret sauce, the ingredient behind all of those decisions.

We really are on a mission. We really are turned outward. We really are after the unchurched. Really.

As I wrote about in *The Rise of the Nones*, our mission is one of the most important values that we hold as a church and one that shapes everything we do.[2] This means that we go to war against the tendency of some churches to pull back and separate themselves into some kind of Christian clique. We never view those outside of the church as the enemy, with an "us versus them" mentality, because that is the exact opposite of the life that Jesus lived. Jesus spent his time with those far from God; he built relationships with them, dined with them in their homes, and went to their parties. This was clearly a life value for him, so it must be what drives the church.

What is killing the church today is having the mission focused on keeping Christians within the church happy, well fed, and growing. Discipleship is continually pitted against evangelism and championed as the endgame for the church. The mission cannot be about us—it must be about those who have not crossed the line of faith.

The problem is, we *like* the mission to be about us. And this has caused a spiritual narcissism to invade the church. You hear it in the words people utter when they walk out of a service and say, "I didn't get anything out of that today." You hear it from the church hoppers, bouncing from one church to the next, when they say, "I really need to go where I'm fed." Please tell me where in the Scriptures you find any talk about that being the mission of the church. Certainly not from the mouth of Jesus, who said:

> The Son of Man did not come to be served, but to serve, and to give his life as a ransom for many. (Matt. 20:28)

> Anyone who wants to be first must be the very last. (Mark 9:35)

> Whoever wants to be first must be slave of all. (Mark 10:44)

> Not my will, but yours be done. (Luke 22:42)

The individual needs and desires of the believer have become the center of attention, which is why most churches have as their primary focus reaching and then serving the already convinced. So the mission isn't making disciples but caring for them. This is an uncomfortable truth. Because almost everybody who follows Christ and almost every gathering of those Christ followers constituting a church say the same thing: "We want to reach the world for Christ."

Yet most don't.

Where's the breakdown?

Jesus knew.

When questioned about his own missional emphasis to those on the outside of faith, he said:

> Who needs a doctor: the healthy or the sick? Go figure out what this Scripture means: "I'm after mercy, not religion." I'm here to invite outsiders, not coddle insiders. (Matt. 9:12–13 Message)

The problem, according to Jesus, are the insiders: Christ followers who have given themselves over to spiritual narcissism and champion that above those who are lost. How does Meck guard against this attitude creeping in? Our secret sauce is simple. It's in a four-word mantra we say to each other all the time around here: "It's not about you." It's about the person who isn't even here yet.

Don't like the new music?

It's not about you.

Don't like the new style of worship?

It's not about you.

Don't like the new dress code?

It's not about you.

Don't like what we're doing with video?

It's not about you.

Don't like the new website?

It's not about you.

It's about them.

Discussion Questions

1. Do you or does your church approach your community with a truly missiological mindset, the same way you would if you were in a new country?

2. When you do cultural research with the goal of reaching someone, do you research what Christians or *non*-Christians think about the topic? Why?

3. What's the average age of staff members and attenders at your church? Are you comfortable with that? If not, what can you do this year to start changing that?

4. What did you think about the notion of targeting men? Evaluate a current service through the eyes of the average male and be honest about how it might come across to them. Did you notice something that should change?

5. Is children's ministry the most well-funded ministry of your church? Do kids who visit your children's ministry beg their parents to bring them back? (Hint: you'll know if they do—their parents will tell you.)

6. When was the last time your church talked about inviting friends and family to a weekend service? What can you do to start building a culture of invitation?

7. How does the approach to discipleship as a third leg differ from your current approach? Does your current discipleship strategy include steps for the newly converted as well as existing believers?

8. When it comes to outreach in your church, are you honestly willing to do whatever it takes to reach the next generation? Are you willing to lose those who can't see that it's not about them?

Afterword

Forget the former things;
    do not dwell on the past.
See, I am doing a new thing!
    Now it springs up; do you not perceive it?

                                    Isaiah 43:18–19

Most pastors and church leaders I know are versed in what it would take to build a cultural bridge. But they don't act on it because they feel like they are caught between a very unique rock and a hard place.

Leaders know the church is not experiencing the growth they desire, particularly among the young and unchurched. They have a solid constituency, but they are older and, most definitely, churched. They are good people, giving people, serving people, but they like the church the way it is. Yet times have changed. Culture has shifted dramatically. Unless they reach the next generation, the church will simply get older and smaller, year by year, until it is a shell of what it once was. But if they attempt to implement some of the things they feel could make a difference, they run the very real risk of alienating their current base of support—the people paying the bills, serving in the nursery, and leading their teams. So they feel stuck. If they don't change, they fear a slow death. If they do change, they fear a quick death. If you fear death, you would rather put it off as long as possible.

Within the challenge presented in this book to reach the next generation is the inherent challenge to have the courage to change. There are many traits one might wish upon pastors and church leaders. Holiness, selflessness, humility . . . but I find that most of them embody such traits. They are good and godly people. So if there is one trait I would wish upon pastors and church leaders around the world, it would be this: *I wish they were more aggressive.*

As Webster's definition puts it, aggressive means "ready or willing to take issue and engage in direct action; full of enterprise and initiative; bold and active; pushing."[1]

When I think of aggressive leaders, I think of

- make-it-happen leaders
- people who don't immediately take no for no
- catalysts for change
- those who take charge in the heat of battle
- upsetters of the status quo
- those with a backbone
- creators of action
- those with righteous anger
- people who are "hungry"
- top-of-the-line, competitive athletes for the kingdom of God

Speaking of athletes, people said that whenever Michael Jordan— arguably the greatest basketball player ever—walked on the court, he was dangerous. He had an aggressive intensity to his game that was threatening to any opponent. I have a framed, limited edition, signed print of Michael Jordan in my office. The picture of Jordan is epic, and the signature is nice, but the words have always captured my attention: "It is a rare person who comes along and raises the standards of excellence, who captures the hearts of many, and who inspires a group of individuals on to achieve the impossible."

May that kind of aggression mark us all. It may just inspire the church to reach the next generation.

Appendix A

Gay Marriage

The following is a talk I delivered at Mecklenburg Community Church titled "Gay Marriage." It was the final installment of a series titled Holy Matrimony. The intent was to address one of the hottest cultural topics of the day, offering a position many outside the Christian faith are diametrically opposed to yet in a way that both explained the historic Christian position and maintained the relationship the church had with those who would be in disagreement. For an MP3 or pdf file of this talk or any other talk given at Meck, visit ChurchAndCulture.org.

Introduction

Today we talk about one of the biggest cultural issues of our day. Gay marriage.

Some of you here today are gay. And you are anxiously awaiting what I'm going to say. Well, first things first. Let me just say a few things to you.

As a follower of Christ, a pastor, and a Christian leader, I want to ask for your forgiveness for the way Christians and Christian organizations have often treated you. I've seen anger—even hatred—among Christians toward gays and lesbians that is repulsive and repugnant to me. And it is repulsive and repugnant to Christ.

There's an us-versus-them mentality as if war has been declared, a spirit manifested that shows nothing but contempt. Even to the point of homophobia—an irrational fear from some.

From those who went public after such events as 9/11 and Hurricane Katrina and said it was God's judgment on homosexuals or on those who support homosexuality.

From those who lead movements to try to get gays fired from public office or to keep them away from fair housing or employment opportunities.

From those who use terms like *fag* or *faggots* or hold up signs at funerals that say, "God hates fags."

Let me publicly apologize to those of you within the homosexual community for that insanity and for the hatred you have felt and even may have experienced from the Christian community.

That has been sin against you, and as a representative Christian, I ask for your forgiveness.

So that's first.

Second, I want you to know that you matter to God. He loves you, he cares about you, and he has a plan for your life. You are one of his precious children.

Your orientation—and yes, I believe for many of you it is your orientation, not simply a random choice you made one day out of the blue—does not make you a second-class person to God.

Third, I want you to know that you matter to me. Pastors and other Christian leaders haven't always made that very clear.

Let me tell you a couple of personal stories, because this is very personal to me.

I remember after I became a Christian, I had a friend in college who was probably the most openly gay guy on the campus. I really liked this guy, and I remember we were walking from class one day and in the middle of a discussion. We were near his apartment, and he asked me if I'd like to come in and have a drink so that we could finish the conversation. So we went inside, and a lot of our conversation was on the spiritual side of things, as I was trying to explain my own decision for Christ, and he was very much in objection to that.

I'll always remember, though, what he said when we finished. I said, "Look, I've got to run—I've got another class to go to."

And he said, "Jim, you're the first Christian who's ever come into my apartment and was just willing to sit and talk with me."

And I remember feeling stunned by this. All he'd ever experienced was rejection.

Fast-forward a couple of years, and I'll never forget receiving a call from a funeral home in southern Indiana where I served as a pastor during my seminary years. A young man who was not connected with a church had died of an AIDS-related illness. Now keep in mind that was twenty-five years ago.

On behalf of the family, the funeral home had contacted pastor after pastor in the area. After finding out the details, each pastor they called had refused even to meet with the family, much less to serve them at the funeral service.

Finally, they got to me—the young seminary kid.

He asked me if I would officiate at the funeral, and I said, "Of course I will."

He then went on to explain how the man had died and wondered if, after hearing the explanation, I would still be willing to do it.

"Of course!" I said.

I can honestly tell you that it never even entered my mind not to serve this family. And I was disgusted with and ashamed of my colleagues for not serving a family during such a time of grief. I knew then, some twenty-five or more years ago, that something was wrong with our attitudes and wrong with our spirits.

So please know, you matter to me. Deeply.

Fourth, I want you to know that you matter to this church. I can't speak for every church, but I can speak for this one.

As a church, from day one, there has been an atmosphere of acceptance for everyone who wants to come and explore what Christ could mean for their lives, including those from the gay community. In fact, we were one of the first churches in the area to try to tackle the AIDS pandemic in Africa. And every time we've discussed homosexuality, our goal has been to do it biblically—but also lovingly, sensitively, and caringly.

I remember, many years ago, the first time I spoke publically on the subject at Meck; we were just over a year old and meeting in an elementary school. We were in a series on issues related to sex and sexuality, and the final installment was going to be on homosexuality. I prayed and worked on that talk like you wouldn't believe because I knew even then that we had a fair number of gay people attending Meck. And I had had several conversations with them about where they stood with their spirituality.

And they mattered to me.

They were people open to Christ but burned by Christians.

They were people who were trying to figure out how the teachings of the Bible meshed with their sexual desires and lifestyles.

They were people trying to figure it all out.

I taught what I felt the Bible said as clearly as I knew how. I tried to explain the Bible's teaching, why it mattered, and what it could mean for all of our lives—gay and straight.

When the talk was over, a woman came up to me and said, "Well, I'm one of your lesbian fans. I had a pretty good idea what you were going to say today. But what I didn't know was how you were going to say it. And I just want to say thank you." And then she hugged me.

I then saw that she had bought about five or six cassette tapes—it was cassette tapes back then—to give to her friends.

You have no idea how much that meant to me and what a personal victory that was for me. She may have disagreed with what I said, but she sensed that our church was marked by love and grace. Not just about the subject but for *her.*

Finally, I want you to know one last thing before we jump in. We're not fixated on this. We're not trying to talk about this every few months. We're not singling this out. We talk about all relevant issues related to sexuality. So we're not trying to single this out, but it is a big issue. And has been for a while. But we're in a series on holy matrimony, so it would be crazy not to talk about it here.

So with that said, let's jump in. I want to approach this in three ways: first, what the Bible says about homosexuality—specifically, homoerotic behavior; second, how that relates to a homosexual orientation; and then third, how all this plays out in relation to gay marriage. So if that sounds like a good road map, let's get started with the Bible.

I. The Bible

To address the issue of homosexuality biblically, we have to begin with God's original design for human sexuality and relationship. This design is found in the book of Genesis, the first book of the Bible, which tells the story of the very creation of humanity. Let me read it:

> The LORD God said, "It is not good for the man to be alone. I will make a helper suitable for him." . . . The LORD God made a woman . . . and brought her to the man. . . . That is why a man leaves his father and mother and is united to his wife, and they become one flesh. Adam and his wife were both naked, and they felt no shame. (2:18, 22, 24–25)

There are four foundational truths to be learned from that passage.

First, that God created sexual identity.

Second, that in making sexual identity, he made human beings male and female. That was the sexual identity he made. After Adam, a man, was created, a helpmate was made that was suitable, appropriate, and correct. For Adam, that person was a woman.

Third, we find that God created sexual intimacy. Not just identity but intimacy.

Finally, that God intended the expression of that sexual intimacy to take place between a man and a woman in the context of marriage. This means that femininity and masculinity are at the heart of God's design. They form the basis for marriage, for the two becoming one. Both genders reflect God's image, and together they reflect and honor God as they join in union with one another. God created men, God created women, God created marriage—so that their differences would complete one another in every conceivable way . . . emotionally, physically, and spiritually.

Which means marriage is more than merely personal. It is more than a contract. And it is much more than tax returns and health insurance. It is a lived-out parable of the principles that undergird the universe. It is the foundational building block of human society.[1] This is why the Bible says that for this reason a man leaves his father and mother and is joined to his wife, and the two are united into one.

Which brings us to homosexuality.

Homosexual behavior departs from God's blueprint in two foundational ways. First, instead of embracing the man-woman design, homosexual behavior embraces a same-sex (man-man, woman-woman) preference as the blueprint for sexual intimacy. Second, at least until recently, it also departed from God's intent for that sexual intimacy to take place within the confines of marriage.

Bracketing off the marriage issue for a moment, let's look at what the Bible has to say about the choice for same-sex sexual intimacy.

In the Old Testament book of Leviticus, the Bible says, "Do not practice homosexuality. . . . It is a detestable sin" (18:22 NLT). Then one chapter later, it adds, "If a man has sex with a man as one does with a woman, both of them have done what is abhorrent" (20:13 Message).

The same is upheld in the New Testament. This is from the book of Romans:

> They traded the truth about God for a lie. . . . Even the women turned against the natural way to have sex and instead indulged in sex with each other. And the men, instead of having normal sexual relationships with women, burned with lust for each other. Men did shameful things with other men. (1:25–27 NLT)

There are other verses, but I won't take time to read them all.

Suffice it to say that every single reference to homosexual behavior in the Bible—Old and New Testament—condemns it. Without question and without qualification. The passages aren't ambiguous, in the way that people might have once looked to the Bible to cherry-pick things and erroneously affirm slavery or make women second-class citizens. You don't have that with these passages.

As Edith Humphrey has written, there are no internal tensions on this matter, and "the moral tradition of the church, from the earliest period into the Reformation and since, has been emphatic: Homoerotic behavior is against the will of God."[2]

But some have still questioned whether what we just read really says what it seems to say. It seems clear enough on the surface, but those who wish to advocate for the legitimacy of a homosexual lifestyle have gone to great pains to discredit each and every biblical reference.

For example, in the passage that we read from Leviticus, they would argue that the book of Leviticus goes on to condemn eating shellfish, cutting your sideburns, and getting tattoos. They would say that it's all ancient religious law shattered by the New Testament fulfillment in Christ, including what it says about homosexuality.

Friends, I'm sorry to put on my old graduate school professor hat, but if I had you in a basic Bible 101 class—like I've taught a thousand times to graduate students and seminary students over the years—I would tell you that is a ridiculous reading of the Scriptures. And it shows a lack of knowledge and, frankly, an ignorance of all this.

You can't write these off as mere cultic practices in ancient Israel and no longer binding on Christians, because that misses out on one of the basic understandings of the Old Testament—namely, that there is a whole body of teaching on ritual uncleanness and a whole body of clear teaching on immoral behavior. One is time bound—caught up with the sacrificial system of the people of Israel. The other is timeless. One describes temple rituals. The other deals with moral laws. They are two different things.

Further, the New Testament condemns homoerotic behavior too!

So when homoerotic behavior is talked about in the Old Testament, it's rooted in creation. In morality. It's not the same as which foods you can eat or what's kosher or not. Just like the prohibitions in the Old Testament against incest, the prohibition against homoerotic behavior is for every age.

Then there are those who take the New Testament to task by saying that while it seems to condemn homosexuality, it's really talking about male prostitutes, not same-sex consensual relationships. The problem with that is that the Greek words used for homosexuality in the New Testament are very clear. They refer to homosexuality of any and every kind.

If you have any doubts about whether the New Testament says what it plainly seems to say, we have books in The Grounds and at The Grounds Posts at all of our campuses that get into this.

So the conclusion remains: God created human beings as male and female. He meant for sexual intimacy to be between a man and a woman alone in the context of marriage. As a result, the Bible sees any departure from that design as outside God's will for our lives, including homosexuality.

II. Orientation

Which brings us to the orientation issue.

Because the biggest argument against what the Bible says really isn't about what the Bible says—that's clear—it's about whether we should accept it. And the biggest reason some give for not accepting it has to do with orientation.

Because people say, "But this is who I am! It's how I was made!" From this, many homosexuals will say that it is unfair, even cruel, to condemn them for pursuing how they naturally are. They say, "Why should I be condemned for following my natural desire! How can God condemn me when he is the one who made me this way?" Or they'll say, "How can the Bible be right when God made me gay?"

Because of this argument, some Christians early on in this cultural debate used to deny that it's really an orientation. That it's all a choice. But, friends, I'm sorry. That's crazy. It's just not true.

Many people who pursue a lifestyle of homosexual behavior didn't set out to be this way; they really do have a very strong tendency toward that behavior. They genuinely have a same-sex attraction. Arguing that is stupid.

Now, can a homosexual orientation be brought to the surface or pursued through various psychological factors or life experiences? Sure. But here's the larger truth: a homosexual orientation is no different from any other orientation someone can have toward a particular lifestyle that may be outside God's will. Someone might have an orientation toward pride, another for chemical addiction, another for gambling or slander, someone else for stealing or lying. All of us have a certain makeup that shapes us and makes us more prone to a particular temptation than others.

It's really dangerous to say, "God made me this way, so it's okay for me to pursue this." Are you sure that God made you that way, or is that just your brokenness? Because this whole world is broken, and we are all sin-stained and sin-soaked. And the world is broken through sin going all the way back to Adam and Eve. So be really careful when you say what God did in terms of how and who you are.

I'm broken.

So play this out: let's say you want to defend pursuing a lifestyle on the basis of orientation. You say, "I do what I do because I am what I am. And because of who I am, this is what I must do." Play that one out. Is this right?

It's certainly not accurate from a psychological point of view. Most would say that who we are is a combination of nature plus nurture. It's how we are put together *and* the choices we make in life.

It's not accurate morally either. If your philosophy is that desire should dictate values, then that means that whatever I desire to do is to be pursued and fulfilled without restraint. Please hang with me on this. If I say that because I have the desire, it must be a legitimate lifestyle, what if my desires are to murder? What if they have to do with molesting young children?

You say, "You're crazy! Nobody in the homosexual community is saying that!"

Of course they're not. But that's beside the point. It is a question of where the philosophy logically leads.

Once you make a philosophy such as this a guiding value system, it applies across the board. You can't pick and choose where you want to apply it. Either desire legitimates behavior, or it doesn't.

What matters is not so much where you are tempted, friends, but what you do with that temptation. I may have moments when in my anger I desire to inflict bodily harm on someone. In fact, a person who struggles with anger is very much oriented toward that very action. But that's very different than it authorizing me to give in to the feeling and act on it.

This is very important. The Bible doesn't condemn anyone for homosexual desire. You need to know that. There's nothing condemning homosexual desire but homosexual practice. But like any other desire outside God's will for our lives, it calls us to resist that temptation.

If someone tells me they're gay, I hardly bat an eye. What I want to know is what choices they are making about how they are living in light of their orientation.

The Bible makes this very clear in the book of James. Let me read its words:

> The temptation to give in to evil comes from us and only us. We have no one to blame but the leering, seducing flare-up of our own lust. Lust gets pregnant, and has a baby: sin! Sin grows up to adulthood, and becomes a real killer. (1:14–15 Message)

The progression there is critical to note.

Temptation comes through our own desire. But just because desire is there doesn't mean what we want to do is okay. Each of us has our own unique areas of weakness, areas where we have desires that aren't of God.

As a straight man, I may have desires for sexual fulfillment outside of marriage with a woman who isn't my wife. But that is no different in God's eyes than the homosexual temptations another person might have. When faced with that temptation, it is up to both of us to choose—to either turn away from the desire or give in to it.

Now the gay person might say, "Well, at least you can get your sexual appetite fulfilled in a marriage. I can't!"

But that's going back and saying that desire is what determines everything. That sexual fulfillment is the one area in our lives that must be in charge and determine everything. You're saying the most important guiding value of your life is making sure you have an orgasm. Really? As if somehow that is the one temptation that should not be fought.

But that's not what the Bible tells us about temptation, no matter what kind it is. Listen to this from the New Testament book of 1 Corinthians:

> The temptations in your life are no different from what others experience. And God is faithful. He will not allow the temptation to be more than you can stand. When you are tempted, he will show you a way out so that you can endure. (10:13 NLT)

It's a really interesting verse. A direct promise that no temptation has seized you that is different from any other temptation any of us face. And that God is faithful. He will provide a way out for you to choose if you so desire.

III. Gay Marriage

Which brings us to gay marriage, which in many ways we've already answered, not just today but throughout this series.

According to the Bible, a homosexual union is in direct contradiction to God's original design in creation. So even if you do have a loving, monogamous relationship with someone of the same sex, it's still a violation of God's design for that relationship to be between a man and a woman in the context of marriage.

But some would say that regardless of where you might stand morally, gay marriage should be endorsed as a fundamental civil right. Even further, that any pledge of love and commitment between two people can only be a positive move, even if you do not support the lifestyle.

But that misses the point. It's not about civil unions. It's about marriage. And wanting this legitimized as a definition of marriage.

Which biblically, you just can't do. Biblically, marriage isn't something we make up or we define. God did it. And it is what it is.

Now if we as a culture want to reduce the idea of marriage to a civil union and make them synonymous—which is what we're essentially doing—then fine. But as a Christian, I can't endorse it.

See, here are the two things that can happen and that are happening: you can lower the definition of marriage to just a civil union or a contract. But biblically, we can't do that—it's so much more. Or you can elevate the civil union and say *that* fulfills God's vision for marriage. And we can't do that either.

Christians are simply being forced to choose another word for the biblical vision. Or certainly give a different definition. Which has really been the point of this series. That things have become so watered down that what we need to talk about isn't marriage but holy matrimony. The biblical idea of what marriage really is about. And it is countercultural, and it is different. Because it's a whole lot more than the right to participate in state-defined benefits.

So do I think Christians should oppose gay-marriage amendments? I think you should vote your conscience. But I will say that I will stand firm, to the end, on the biblical definition of what marriage should be in our culture. And even if I'm the last lone voice crying out in the wilderness, I will be that voice.

IV. Final Pastoral Words

Now having said all of this, I have two closing pastoral words.

First, I know that some of you are instantly thinking that all this acceptance talk that I started off with just got ripped away from you. You will say this is not accepting at all. And here's why. Because to you, the only acceptance that you will accept as acceptance is affirmation. Approval. If you don't approve, if you don't affirm, then you don't accept.

Okay, you are now being as unfair to someone like me as Christians used to be unfair to you.

You rightfully rebelled against those who wanted to single out and criminalize your lifestyle, but now you want to criminalize those who disagree with your lifestyle and say that the only way you can have acceptance and tolerance is if I affirm you.

Well, I'm going to push back, because that is a screwed-up idea of tolerance. And I've talked about this before. There are three kinds of tolerance.

The first is legal tolerance. This has to do with our basic first amendment rights to believe what we want to believe. There is nothing in the Christian stance on gay marriage that goes against that. In fact, the Bible is a great advocate of legal tolerance.

The second is social or cultural tolerance. This is accepting someone else as who they are regardless of what they believe. Loving them, caring about them, being open to them relationally. There is nothing in all of this against that either. If Jesus stood for anything, it was open, loving acceptance of others as people who mattered to God.

The third is intellectual tolerance. This is accepting what someone believes as right regardless of what you believe or think is right. And it's only in that sense that the Christian stance on gay marriage would be considered intolerant, because Jesus didn't believe that everything and everyone was right. The Bible clearly holds to the idea that there is right and wrong, true and false.

But that's the way most of us feel, isn't it? Think about it. Do any of us really believe in rampant intellectual tolerance? That there is no right, there is no wrong, it doesn't really matter?

Perhaps someone came up to you and said, "I believe that the best way to improve the performance of your car is to pour sand into the gas tank." Now, can I be tolerant of that person—legally and relationally—without buying into what he says? Of course!

I can say, "You know what, I think you have every right to pour sand into your car. It's your car—and I'm not going to get all worked up to try to stop you legally from doing it. Have at it. And if you do, I'm still gonna come over to your house this weekend so that we can watch the finale of *Breaking Bad*. This doesn't impact us socially at all. You're still my friend."

But being legally tolerant and socially tolerant doesn't mean I'm going to be intellectually tolerant. I'm still going to tell you that I don't agree. I'm not going to put sand in my car, and I don't mind telling you that, much less advising other drivers that I don't think they should either. And I'll go further. I will resist you trying to make it so that I affirm sand in the car as an option or that somehow I get roped into putting sand into mine.

If that's the endgame here—where it's not just about acceptance or legality but the desire to criminalize any denunciation and force others to participate or affirm—well then, friends, we're into a whole different territory.

And I'll say to my gay friends, "I hope that you can see that's where this is heading, and I hope that you'll join me in denouncing it."

So it is one thing to be against homosexuality and to affirm that the Bible rejects the practice of same-sex lifestyles—which I believe it does—but it is another to be against homosexuals—which I do not embrace. And I can be accepting of you, loving toward you, and hold to that. And I hope we all can uphold that together.

Here's my second pastoral word, to all of us. This sin is no greater than any other sin. The struggle of gays in being attracted to the same sex is no different than my struggle with anger, or with impatience, or with gluttony. And when people give in to it, it is no worse than any other sin. All sin, at its heart, is rebellion against God.

Now it's true that sexual sins are particularly destructive to our lives. But that's true no matter what the sexual sin is—whether it's adultery or an addiction to pornography. All of us are broken sexually. We all need healing and health, wholeness and redemption.

If you are gay, the ultimate issue is not the gay lifestyle. My primary issue as your pastor is not your homoerotic lifestyle. That's not the starting point. The first and most important issue is not that you straighten yourself out in this area and then come to Christ. The most important issue is your relationship with Christ. That you come to Christ first and then see how he applies to your sexuality and sexual choices.

Conclusion

Just like the rest of us are doing. We all have the same disease. We're all being treated for sin-sickness. We're all in some kind of recovery. So whatever you brought with you today, you're not alone. And we do not condemn you. You are no different from any of the rest of us struggling with areas of temptation and desire. And we've all failed in those areas.

But Christ is working on all of us.

Meck is nothing but a colossal collection of moral foul-ups. Really, if you're new here, I have to warn you—you're in some bad company here. We have sins of pride, greed, pornography, self-righteousness, lying, stealing, adultery, insensitivity to others. . . .

But through the power of Christ, there is hope for all of us.

But here's what else you need to know. We want to expose those areas in our lives—not deny them or rationalize them away. We want to run to what the Bible says, not to find loopholes or ways to justify or denounce what it says. Not in a way that condemns but in a way that transforms. We want to discover our junk, go to God for forgiveness, and become increasingly changed people.

So our invitation?

Join us.

Join me—the chief of sinners. But oh if you only knew what I was like before Christ started to work in my life.

So that's all I have to say on this one.

Let's stand for a closing prayer.

Appendix B

Map of the Spiritual World

The following is a talk I delivered at Mecklenburg Community Church titled "Map of the Spiritual World." It was the first installment of a series titled Paranormal. The intent was to tap into the strong interest and belief in the supernatural among post-Christians. For an MP3 or pdf file of this talk or any other talk given at Meck, visit ChurchAndCulture.org.

Introduction

Welcome to Meck and a new series on the paranormal. And there's a reason we're tackling this besides the fact that it's October and Halloween is just around the corner. It's because polls are coming out showing that when it comes to the world of spirits, we're becoming big believers.

A new study just came out in the United Kingdom that found more than half of the entire population believes in the supernatural world—ghosts, spirits, psychic powers, etc.—a dramatic rise from the last time it was charted just four years ago.

The paranormal has become big business, with the popularity of television shows like *Most Haunted* and the spread of ghost walks around supposedly haunted parts of city centers. English Heritage and the National Trust have both started to identify which of their properties are said to be occupied by ghosts in order to attract more visitors.

It's a similar story in the United States. Recent polls show about half of us believe in ghosts or that the spirit of a dead person can come back in certain places or situations.[1]

And Hollywood is paying very close attention. Beyond the rage of the Twilight series of books and movies, NBC is getting ready to unveil a $2 million per episode *Downton Abbey*-ish series on Dracula. Fox's main show for the fall is an updated take on Ichabod Crane and the Headless Horseman. The second installment of the Insidious series, which came out just a few weeks ago, claimed the top spot at the box office. And then there are all the TV shows like *Ghost Hunters, Ghost Adventures, Ghost Stories, Celebrity Ghost Stories, Long Island Medium, The Dead Files* . . . And coming soon are such shows as CMT's *Voodoo Paranormal*, TLC's *Cajun Paranormal*, and my personal favorite, Syfy's *Meatloaf Rocks the Paranormal*.

There are even phone apps that supposedly act as a ghost meter and aid in detecting ghosts.

Bottom line: we are interested in the paranormal. The word itself means psychic or mental phenomena outside the range of the normal, or what used to be called the world of the occult.

The word *occult* just means that which is hidden or secret beyond the range of ordinary human knowledge or below the surface of normal life. Used in that sense, it's almost a neutral term. And that's the way most people want to use the word. They want all of this to be something neutral, something benign. A supernatural phenomena. Fun for movies or fun for a tour or fun for ghost stories.

But when we say that something is paranormal, or occultic, is that really all it is? Just something fun or intriguing . . . maybe this impersonal psychic force or energy field out there that is kinda fun to play with.

What about séances and witchcraft, horoscopes and Ouija boards, psychics and mediums, tarot cards and palm readings, and most insidious of all, the Duke Blue Devils?

Think about it. Where does God fit in, and angels, and the spiritual side of things, and life after death?

That's what we're going to explore in this series: the nature of the supernatural world, the world of spirits, their interaction with human beings, and what actually falls into that world that we may never have realized. And along the way, we'll find out whether it's really that benign.

So let's get started with a map of the spiritual world, because the Bible gives us one—a kind of "who's who," a "what's what," and a "where's where."

I think this is going to be eye opening and certainly an important foundation for things that we'll be talking about in the weeks to come.

I. The Spiritual Realm

Let's start off with the Bible's teaching, which says that there is, in fact, another dimension—a spiritual, or supernatural, world. And it is inhabited by beings, by creatures, and by intense activity. And they, and their activity, can interact with life on planet Earth. And when they do, it is paranormal.

For example, in the New Testament book of Ephesians, the apostle Paul writes these words:

> Be strong in the Lord and in his mighty power. Put on the full armor
> of God, so that you can take your stand against the devil's schemes.
> For our struggle is not against flesh and blood, but against the rulers,
> against the authorities, against the powers of this dark world and
> against the spiritual forces of evil in the heavenly realms. Therefore
> put on the full armor of God, so that when the day of evil comes,
> you may be able to stand your ground. (6:10–13)

Now that's worth unpacking.

We've just been told in that passage that not only is there a
spiritual realm, but also not all of it is good. And there is conflict,
even open war. And at stake are God's purposes and the battle
between God and the enormous spiritual forces arrayed against
him. In terms of ultimate reality, this is the war, this is the conflict,
this is the battle that matters the most. Not the ones that make
the news—not chemical weapons in Syria, not the saber rattling
of North Korea, not the Republicans versus Democrats in budget
showdowns. The real conflict is the battle against the spiritual
forces that war against God in heaven.

And in the passage we just read, that evil realm is described.
Did you catch it? Take another look at some of the excerpts:

> . . . the rulers, . . . the authorities, . . . the powers of this dark
> world . . . and . . . the spiritual forces of evil in the heavenly realms.
> (Eph. 6:12)

So what are those powers? What are those forces? What is out
there besides God and us?

Well, there is a class of beings you've heard about your whole life
but may have never really understood. Let me introduce them to you.

John Paton, a pioneer missionary in the New Hebrides Islands,
tells how one night hostile natives surrounded his mission head-
quarters. They were intent on burning the Patons out and killing
them. John and his wife prayed all during that terror-filled night
that God would deliver them. When daylight came, they were

amazed to see that not only had they survived the night, but every one of their attackers had left.

A year later, the chief of the tribe gave his life to Christ. John, remembering what had happened, asked the chief what had kept him and his men from burning down his house and killing him.

The chief replied in surprise, "Well, who were all those men you had with you there?"

John said, "There were no men there, just me and my wife."

The chief said, "No, there were many men there standing guard. Hundreds of big men in shining garments with drawn swords in their hands. They circled the entire mission station so that we were terrified and afraid to attack, so we fled."[2]

Both men agreed it could only have been angels.

So what are angels?

II. Five Things to Know about Angels

There are five basic things to know about angels. Let me walk you through these.

A. Angels Are Creatures Created by God

First, angels are creatures created by God. They are not gods themselves or in any way on equal footing with God. For example, the 148th Psalm in the Bible says:

> Praise the LORD. . . .
> Praise him, all his angels. . . .
> Let them praise the name of the LORD,
>   for at his command they were created. (vv. 1–2, 5)

As created beings of God, angels have intelligence and a will. They are moral creatures and, like us, can choose either to obey God or to disobey God.

B. Angels Are Not Human

But second, they are not human. They are spirits. The Bible says in the book of Hebrews: "Angels [are] ministering spirits sent to serve those who will inherit salvation" (1:14).

They do not have physical bodies as we have, though when they interact with humans they can, and often do, assume a human form.

C. Angels Are Powerful

A third thing about angels is that they are powerful, far more powerful than we are. In 2 Peter, the Bible simply says, "Angels . . . are stronger and more powerful" than men (2:11).

But that's putting it mildly.

In another section of the Bible, the book of 2 Kings in the Old Testament, the Bible says that one angel was sent to destroy 185,000 Assyrians. One angel was enough.

And in the book of Revelation, when it talks about the world being destroyed at the end of time, it is done largely through the power of seven angels as they carry out the commands of God. That's all it will take—seven. To destroy the entire known universe and created reality. Seven are more than enough.

D. There Are a Lot of Them

Fourth, there are a lot of them. While we have the names of only a few of them—such as Gabriel, Michael, . . . Clarence—just seeing if you're paying attention.

Jesus made reference to being able to call down twelve legions of angels if he needed them. A legion in the Roman army varied from between 3,000 to 6,000 men, so Jesus's reference alluded to anywhere from 36,000 to 72,000 angels. Now that was figurative language, but it still tells us that Jesus understood there to be thousands upon thousands of angels. So the point is that there are vast numbers of them.

For example, the book of Hebrews speaks of "thousands upon thousands of angels in joyful assembly" (12:22). And in the book of Revelation, the apostle John writes of his God-given vision of heaven at the end of time with these words: "I looked and heard the voice of many angels, numbering thousands upon thousands, and ten thousand times ten thousand" (5:11).

So while we don't know the exact number, we know it's a lot.

E. There Are Different Kinds of Angels

Finally, there are different kinds of angels. For example, there are angels called cherubim, which seem to be the highest order, or at least those closest to the throne of God. And then there are angels called seraphim. And there are archangels, which seem to be the most powerful. And who knows how many other kinds the Bible just doesn't detail. It seems to be a highly structured realm and order.

But the most important separation between the angels is this: there are good angels and there are bad angels. Not all of the angels that God created have stayed loyal to God. Some rebelled, lost their place and holy condition, and now oppose the work and will of God. Which is why in the Bible, the writer of the book of Jude says, "I remind you of those angels who were once pure and holy but turned to a life of sin" (1:6 TLB).

And that is what a demon is—a fallen angel who chose to rebel. Nothing more and nothing less.

Knowing about the existence of bad angels is important, because the Bible says that demons have one and only one purpose: to oppose the work and will of God—both in this world and in your life.

And their main strategy is clear. It is deception—to be seen as anything but truly evil, or demonic. In fact, their strategy is to try to appear as good angels, good beings, good forces in order to lead us away from God. For example, in 2 Corinthians, the Bible warns us that "Satan himself masquerades as an angel of light" (11:14).

That is why the Bible gives us the litmus test. It's found in the book of Galatians, where the apostle Paul writes:

> Evidently some people are throwing you into confusion and are trying to pervert the gospel of Christ. But even if we or an angel from heaven should preach a gospel other than the one we preached to you, let him be under God's curse! As we have already said, so now I say again: If anybody is preaching to you a gospel other than what you accepted, let him be under God's curse! (1:7–9)

Which is why the Bible gives this advice in the first letter of John: "Dear friends, do not believe every spirit, but test the spirits to see whether they are from God" (4:1).

Now let's talk about Satan.

III. About Satan

Satan is known by many names—the devil, Lucifer, the evil one, the tempter, the deceiver, the adversary, and the prince of darkness.

The Bible teaches that Satan is a fallen angel—no more, no less—who chose to enter into rebellion against God. He was probably an archangel, among the most powerful of all the angels—on line with Michael the archangel. And according to the book of Revelation, it seems he led at least one-third of the angels with him in rebellion (see Rev. 12:4).

The heart of his fall was pride. In Isaiah, this is how his downfall is described:

> How you have fallen from heaven,
>   morning star, son of the dawn!
> You have been cast down to the earth,
>   you who once laid low the nations!
> You said in your heart,
>   "I will ascend to the heavens;

> I will raise my throne
> > above the stars of God;
> I will sit enthroned on the mount of assembly,
> > on the utmost heights of Mount Zaphon.
> I will ascend above the tops of the clouds;
> > I will make myself like the Most High."
> But you are brought down to the realm of the dead,
> > to the depths of the pit. (14:12–15)

Now even if he was an archangel, there are a few things worth remembering:

He's not all-knowing or all-powerful.

He's not God or even close to being God.

He's not the evil twin brother of Jesus.

The Bible says that he is an angel who fell.

So don't fall prey to a dualist view of good and evil that has good and evil being equal, or Satan being as powerful as God. That's not at all the state of things. The Bible says that Satan gave in to pride and wanted to sit where God sits. He rebelled against God and declared all-out war. The Bible doesn't go into detail as to why God allowed Satan to be in opposition to him. All we know is that God has allowed him to exercise his free will and to be in rebellion, just as he has allowed us to exercise our free will and make our choices.

But he is to be taken very, very seriously. And if you have any doubt about that, all you have to do is look at what Jesus had to say about him. Because Jesus believed in him and took him very, very seriously. He didn't think he was a myth. He didn't think he was a figment of someone's imagination or some cartoon character with a red suit and pointed tail. He didn't think he was a mere projection of our minds in order to explain away the mysteries of evil.

Jesus believed and knew Satan to be a real, live spiritual being and wanted his followers to take him seriously as well. And not just to take him seriously but to know some things about him.

Here's what Jesus wanted us to know.

A. *He's a Murderer*

First, Jesus said that Satan is a murderer. In one of the four biographies of the life of Jesus, the New Testament book of John, Jesus says, "The devil . . . was a murderer from the beginning" (8:44).

Jesus did not think the devil was cute. He did not think he was just a little bit naughty. Jesus said that Satan is a being who is totally evil and malicious, someone who kills and destroys, someone who is absolutely and totally opposed to God and all that is of God. A murderer—and one *from the beginning*.

In the Garden of Eden, he led Adam and Eve to rebellion against God. He knew that their rebellion would lead to spiritual death, to separation from God. And no sooner had he done that than he went to work on inciting physical murder as well between their sons, Cain and Abel. And he's been on a murderous rampage ever since.

Who do you think most celebrated the killings at the Washington Navy Yard? Sandy Hook? Aurora, Colorado? Fort Hood? Virginia Tech? 9/11?

Who do you think celebrates every single life that goes to the grave divorced from a saving life in Christ and faces an eternity in hell?

Who do you think celebrates that?

The great murderer of all murderers.

B. *He's a Liar*

Second, Jesus called him a liar. Listen to these words of Jesus also recorded in John's biography: Satan does not hold "to the truth, for there is no truth in him. When he lies, he speaks his native language, for he is a liar and the father of lies" (8:44).

Did you know that's where we get our word *devil*? It's from the Greek word *diabolos*, which means "slanderer." Someone who spreads lies and half-truths about someone or something in order to get others to think or do the wrong things.

And the word *Satan* literally means "accuser." Again, one who brings hostile, false accusations against someone else.

Jesus said that Satan is a destructive, malicious, evil liar whose lying is intended to tear down, attack, and destroy the reputation of truth. And do you know what his biggest lie is? His most essential, foundational lie? The lie he's been working on since the Garden of Eden for every human life?

It's that bad is good. That single lie is at the heart of all of his deception:

- that wrong is right
- that what is false is true
- that what is harmful is healthy
- that what is immoral is moral
- that what is cruel is kind
- that what is unjust is just
- that choosing to sin, to go against God, to live apart from God, is best and even virtuous—logical, rational, smart

C. He's a Destroyer

The third thing that Jesus said about Satan is found in a story Jesus told. It's an important story, so let me read it to you.

One day Jesus told a story in the form of a parable to a large crowd that had gathered from many towns to hear him: "A farmer went out to plant his seed. As he scattered it across his field, some seed fell on a footpath, where it was stepped on, and the birds ate it.

Other seed fell among rocks. It began to grow, but the plant soon wilted and died for lack of moisture. Other seed fell among thorns that grew up with it and choked out the tender plants. Still other seed fell on fertile soil. This seed grew and produced a crop that was a hundred times as much as had been planted!" . . .

"This is the meaning of the parable: The seed is God's word. The seeds that fell on the footpath represent those who hear the message, only to have the devil come and take it away from their hearts and prevent them from believing and being saved. The seeds on the rocky soil represent those who hear the message and receive it with joy. But since they don't have deep roots, they believe for a while, then they fall away when they face temptation. The seeds that fell among the thorns represent those who hear the message, but all too quickly the message is crowded out by the cares and riches and pleasures of this life. And so they never grow into maturity. And the seeds that fell on the good soil represent honest, good-hearted people who hear God's word, cling to it, and patiently produce a huge harvest." (Luke 8:4–8, 11–15 NLT)

Now in that story, Jesus tells us the third thing about Satan: that he is a destroyer. He wants to keep everyone away from the life that comes through receiving the truth of God's message through Christ. And if somebody does hear the message of Christ, if they do get a good, solid dose of spiritual truth, his number one goal is to try to snatch it away—to do anything possible to have them reject it or dismiss it. He wants to steal it from their hearts. And if he can't do that, if he can't get them to walk away from it, then according to Jesus's story, he'll just try to make sure they don't do anything with it. That they don't ever take it very seriously and that they are these casual believers. That it never takes root, that it becomes just another phase or a passing fad. Or, as Jesus told it, that they let their life just crowd it out, marginalize it, so that it doesn't have any room to become significant.

That's the character and intent of the evil one.

Now the choice to go along with what Satan tempts us with is ours and ours alone. That's why this was so important to Jesus for people to understand. He wants us to be on the lookout for his schemes, to be aware of his agenda, so that we are not blindsided and willing to go along with the temptation. Because Satan will do everything he can to hide his efforts.

It reminds me of one of the most fascinating books you'll ever read. It's by C. S. Lewis, and it's called *The Screwtape Letters*. Go by The Grounds or any Grounds Post at our campuses and get a copy. It's one of the most intriguing books you'll ever read. It's a fictitious record of a series of letters between a senior devil named Screwtape, from a highly organized hell, to his nephew Wormwood, a junior devil, in regard to the art of winning over a young man's soul, his "patient" on earth.

In one of those letters, Wormwood wants to know if he should keep his "patient" in ignorance of his existence. Screwtape writes back and says, "Our policy . . . is to conceal ourselves."

Then in a later letter, Screwtape writes to Wormwood about why that's the best policy:

> The goal is to lead the human to make small steps away from God, to begin to believe small lies, as opposed to leading the man to spectacular wickedness all at once which he may all too easily see as truly evil and turn from it.

Then the senior demon, Screwtape, writes these words:

> The only thing that matters is the extent to which you separate the man from the Enemy [the enemy, of course, being God]. It does not matter how small the sins are, provided that their cumulative effect is to edge the man away from the Light out into the Nothing. . . . The safest road to Hell is the gradual one—the gentle slope, soft underfoot, without sudden turnings, without milestones, without signposts.[3]

D. He's Defeated

So are you with me so far?

Jesus said that Satan is real and is utterly, totally evil. He's also a liar and bent on destroying your exploration and growth in the Christian faith.

Now if you're like me, none of what Jesus has had to say so far has been very good news. But fortunately, that's not all that Jesus had to say. This is what he told his followers the week before his crucifixion:

> "The time for judging this world has come, when Satan, the ruler of this world, will be cast out. And when I am lifted up from the earth, I will draw everyone to myself." He said this to indicate how he was going to die. (John 12:31–33 NLT)

The last and most significant thing that Jesus said about Satan is that *he is defeated*, and that it was his death on the cross that did it.

You see, Satan wants each and every person to die separated from God, unforgiven for their sins. He wants them to face the full penalty. He wants them in hell. That's the depth of his hatred.

He knows that the penalty for the sin in our lives is death. He knows that if the sin problem is not addressed, if it's not remedied, then the only result is eternal separation from God. So he wants everyone to die in their sins without having a relationship with God as Leader and certainly not as Forgiver. That's where the word *saved* comes from. He doesn't want anyone saved from the penalty of their disobedience.

But that's where the cross comes in. Jesus willingly went to the cross and as One who knew no sin, laid down his life for your sin. And my sin. He paid the penalty. He went to war on this one.

And by rising from the dead three days later, Jesus made it clear that death does not have to have the final victory. He's above the spiritual world, the angelic world, the supernatural world. He's Lord of all.

And not only that, you can receive forgiveness for your sins, walk in a relationship with God, and when you die, enter into life eternal. By accepting what Christ did for you on the cross, in your place, you can receive forgiveness for your sin.

By his death and resurrection, Jesus conquered the powers of Satan over sin and death and hell. And at the end of time, when Jesus returns, Satan will be judged along with everyone else. The victory will be complete.

But in between the now and the not yet, Satan is alive and well on planet Earth. Defeated but still loose. The time of great choice and free will for us all—where Satan tries to keep as many from God as possible and seeks to not only deceive but also destroy.

IV. The World of the Occult

So there you have it, a map of the supernatural world.

On the one side, you have God and his faithful angels.

On the other side, the world of the paranormal or the occult, which is the world of Satan and his demons, or the world of the angels who fell. Rebelled. A world you do not want any part of.

These are the only two worlds. These are the only two forces. These are the only two sets of beings. There isn't anything else. One of them is good; the other is evil.

There are a lot of ways, sadly, that Satan and his team seduce us to engage the evil side—to open our lives to it and to invite it in, without even knowing it. And when we do, whether we are aware of it or not, we are engaging the forces of darkness. We are connecting with Satan and his demons. We are willfully opening up the doors of our lives to their presence and activity. And they will enter. And nothing could be more dangerous.

Initially, it might seem benign, even innocent—for as the Bible says, he positions himself as an angel of light—but then the evil engulfs you. And it's even more than playing with fire—it's dousing yourself with gasoline and then lighting the match.

We talk of possession and oppression, attack and opposition, affliction and warfare. Well, this is how it starts. You open yourself up to the dark side. Not the timid, tame idea of *Star Wars* but the wide-open torrent, wildfire, deluge, devastation, tsunami, cataclysm, infestation . . . of Satan and his demons. It is spiritual suicide. And nothing could be more terrifying. And if you've ever encountered the demonic, which I have, nothing is more terrifying.

Which is why what we're going to be talking about next week will be so critical, which is the most common ways people—often without even knowing it—are playing with the occult and inviting Satan and his demons into their lives. You don't want to miss it.

Let's stand for a closing prayer.

Appendix C

Why Believe in God?

The following is a talk I delivered at Mecklenburg Community Church titled "Why Believe in God?" It was the second installment of a series titled Why Believe. The intent was to address reasons for belief in an age of skepticism and also to build on what still constitutes common ground, such as Generation Z's sense of awe and wonder at the cosmos and how they feel it might reasonably point to God. For an MP3 or pdf file of this talk or any other talk given at Meck, visit ChurchAndCulture.org.

▬▬▬

Introduction

Welcome to Meck!

We're getting ready to enter the big summer movie season, with the latest Avengers film starting things off in just a few weeks. So let's play some movie trivia.[1] I'll throw up the questions, and see if you can guess the answer. And just guess in your head. Here we go:

1. Who was the first female monster to appear in a movie?

    A. Godzilla

    B. the bride of Frankenstein

    C. the Mummy (Get it?!)

    D. Kim Kardashian

Got your pick?

Answer: the bride of Frankenstein.

2. What was the first movie that was ever given the title "blockbuster"?

    A. *Star Wars*

    B. *Gone with the Wind*

    C. *Jaws*

    D. *Dumb and Dumber 3*

Answer: *Jaws.*

3. Which of these actors once had a job polishing coffins?

    A. Marlon Brando

    B. Sean Connery

    C. Robert Pattinson

    D. Bela Lugosi

Answer: Sean Connery.

4. Who has the most nominations for an Oscar in movie history?

    A. Jack Nicholson

    B. Laurence Olivier

    C. Paul Newman

    D. Justin Bieber

Answer: Jack Nicholson (twelve times).

Okay, one last one.

    5. What do the following six actors all have in common—
    beyond, of course, that they're all actors: Daniel Radcliffe,
    Julianne Moore, Keira Knightley, Ian McKellen, Hugh Lau-
    rie, and Jodie Foster?
        A. They've all been nominated for an Oscar.
        B. They've all had the same director in a film.
        C. They've all been in a movie that earned over $50 million
           at the box office.
        D. They're all atheists.
Answer: They're all atheists.

Last week we kicked off a series called Why Believe with a look at why believe in Jesus and, specifically, his resurrection. Today we're going to look at why even believe in God.

Granted, not many people are card-carrying atheists. But there are a fair number of agnostics, and you might be one of them. An agnostic doesn't necessarily reject God as much as the possibility of knowing.

But do you have to be agnostic? Is it possible to dig into whether or not God exists and come away saying, "It makes more sense to believe in God than not to believe in God"?

Let's find out. Let's look at some of the reasons why the idea of God is so intellectually plausible—so intellectually compelling—to a lot of people.

I. Cause and Effect

Let's start with the cosmological reason, or more commonly known as cause and effect. This reason for believing in God rests on a simple, commonsense question: You look around at the world and ask, "How did this happen?" It was caused by something. What was that cause?

The universe had a beginning. Anything that has a beginning must have been *begun*. It couldn't have started itself—it had to have been caused by something else.

And going all the way back, what caused everything in the beginning had to have been itself uncaused. In other words, there had to have been a First, Uncaused Cause.

Think of it this way. If you see a row of dominoes, and they are falling over, you know that somewhere, somehow the first domino got pushed.

What about the universe? It's going. Who, or what, pushed it?

For a long time, skeptics rejected the idea of cause and effect as an argument for God because they didn't think the universe had a beginning. The idea was the universe was eternal in nature; it didn't have a start date where, prior to that date, nothing existed.

That's not what most scientists think anymore.

Most of us are familiar with the second law of thermodynamics, which says the universe is running out of usable energy. If it is running down, then it could not be eternal and must have at one time been given a start. If something is winding down, it must have sometime been wound up.

But what has really laid the eternal universe theory to rest is the idea of the Big Bang. The idea of the Big Bang was first put forward by Dr. Edwin Hubble, the one we named the Hubble Space Telescope after. His theory was that at one time all matter was packed into a dense mass at temperatures of many trillions of degrees. Then about 13.8 billion years ago, there was a huge explosion. And from that explosion, all of the matter that today forms our planets and stars was born. That explosion created the universe as we know it.

Hubble's idea was later confirmed through what was then called the discovery of the century. On April 24, 1992, the Cosmic Background Explorer satellite, better known as COBE, gave stunning confirmation of the hot Big Bang creation event through its analysis of cosmic microwave background radiation.

Then, in 2014, a team of scientists working in Antarctica found what has been called the smoking gun of the universe's expansion through the Big Bang. They discovered the gravitational waves that are the evidence of expansion.[2]

If you don't think this has sent shock waves through the world of cosmology, take a look at this.

———

Big Bang/Hubble video
https://youtu.be/vNH040mOJcA

———

So what does this mean?

Well, it means we have a creation event.

But do we have a God?

Science can't answer that. That's way above its pay grade. But it sure has led a lot of people to think that way. Here's why.

If the universe could not have come into being by itself from nothing, because it is a scientific impossibility that absolute nothingness could produce anything—I mean, the original matter had to come from somewhere; and if the universe isn't eternal—there really was a creation event through the Big Bang—then who made it bang? And where did the stuff that got banged come from?

You can't not ask those questions! You can't dismiss the idea of God in relation to the origin of the universe by saying it was the Big Bang. Because you can't have a Big Bang without a Big Banger!

And as leading physicist Alan Guth at MIT has written, even if you could come up with a theory that would account for the creation of something from nothing through the laws of physics, you'd still have to account for the origin of the laws of physics! Where do they come from?

All of this makes the idea of a creation through a Creator not only compatible with science but almost demanded by it. So when you look back to what the Bible says in Genesis 1:1, that "in the beginning God created the heavens and the earth," it adds up! One who was without beginning, one who stands outside our boundaries of space and time, created.

As the New Testament book of Romans adds:

> What can be known about God is plain to them. . . . Ever since God created the world, his invisible qualities, both his eternal power and his divine nature, have been clearly seen; they are perceived in the things that God has made. (1:19–20 GNT)

II. Design and Order

So that's one reason to believe in God.

Another reason has to do with design. The essence of this reason to believe is found in a very important question: How do you account for the intricate design of the universe?

This idea is an old one, which tells you of its power. It was first articulated by the Greek philosopher Plato but was popularized many years later by William Paley. The thinking is as follows:

- All designs imply a designer.
- If you find a watch, you would understandably assume a watchmaker; if you see a building, you would assume an architect; if you view a painting, you would take for granted that there was a painter.
- And the greater the complexity of the design and order of something, the more a designer begs to be considered.

I once heard it put this way: It's one thing to see a logjam and wonder if there was a beaver behind it; it's another to see the Hoover Dam and question whether there was intentionality and purpose behind its creation.

Or think of it this way. Imagine you came upon a space shuttle in the middle of the desert. You *could* reason that it came together by chance, that the metal was flung together by way of a chaotic sandstorm, that the instruments and panels and wings were brought together by a freak accident of nature. But it is highly unlikely that this would be your *first* thought. If you came upon a space shuttle in the desert, your initial thought would likely be that someone made it and landed it there.

There is staggering design and order to the universe, so staggering that it compels many people to consider a great Designer of the universe. Even the Bible suggests this as a reason for faith in God. Let me read an example from the Psalms:

> The heavens are telling the glory of God; they are a marvelous display of his craftsmanship. Day and night they keep on telling about God. Without a sound or word, silent in the skies, their message reaches out to all the world. (19:1–4 TLB)

But this design is not just about the cosmos but also about the intricately ordered wonders of the human body, the most ordered mechanism on the planet.

Now, you might be thinking, "Hold on. Doesn't that bring up evolution, and doesn't that disprove God?"

No.

Where are you getting that?

If the theory of evolution were ever 100 percent proved, beyond any shadow of a doubt, it would be a huge reason to believe in God.

III. Evolution

Here's why.

First, it's absolutely true that the Bible tells us that God created human beings. Here's what Genesis says:

So God created mankind in his own image, in the image of God
he created him; male and female he created them. . . . The LORD
God formed a man from the dust of the ground and breathed into
his nostrils the breath of life, and the man became a living being.
(1:27; 2:7)

So without a doubt, the Bible says that we were created by a
Creator. That we were wonderfully and carefully designed. That
the entire creative process was miraculously and supernaturally
generated and guided by God.

But it doesn't say *how*, except in a literary, poetic way—using
phrases like "the dust of the earth" and "the breath of life." Which
doesn't exactly sound like it was trying to be a biology text.

So we're told *that* God did it but not how.

Evolution is one of the leading theories in science for the "how."
Which is fine. If God used evolution, so be it. That doesn't mean
there wasn't an original Adam and Eve whom God breathed actual
souls into at the end of the process to mark the beginning of the
human race as we know it today. In fact, if you know much about
evolution, if it's true, it would take an outside force, an outside
intelligence of some kind, to explain it.

The theory of evolution calls for leaps and mutations to overcome massive unexplained gaps that almost scream for an intelligent Designer guiding and helping the process.

Just think about the time issue. If the age of the earth is about 4.6
billion years—which is the current, best estimate of science—and
we have evidence of abundant and complex life 3.5 billion years
ago—which we do—then that means there was only about 170
million years for the earth to cool from its initial formation and
for all of evolution to have taken place. Just 170 million years. And
that simply isn't enough time—by anyone's calculations—for all
of evolution to have taken place.

In fact, noted astronomer Sir Fred Hoyle has written that if you
would compute the time required to get all two hundred thousand

amino acids for one human cell to come together by chance, it would be about 293.5 times the estimated age of the earth.[3] It would be like having the working dynamics of an iPod, iPhone, iPad, and smart watch all instantly created—by chance—through a single explosion in a computer warehouse. It's almost crazy to think about.

So if evolution is true, there is the need for some kind of outside, guiding, enhancing force to speed it along in the time frame of the age of the earth.

But that's not all.

Even if there was enough time, and even if you buy into all of these mutations and leaps filling all of the gaps—just like with the Big Bang—you need something, or Someone, to have gotten it started. At least, that's what we're finding through molecular biology.

Think about something like the human eye. According to evolutionary theory, it would have started with a simple, light-sensitive spot and then evolved to what we see with today. The problem is that when we finally got to the point where we were able to study life at the molecular level, we found it wasn't simple. We found it was irreducibly complex. Which means something, or Someone, had to create those first complex systems, that first light-sensitive spot.

And if I just lost you, let's see if this video will clear it up.

▬▬▬

Irreducible Complexity/Michael Behe
https://youtu.be/cWorialvq2s

▬▬▬

So evolution doesn't war against believing in God. In fact, believing in both is called believing in theistic evolution—meaning that God created and chose evolution as the means.

People who believe in God simply point to the idea that naturalistic evolution—meaning an evolutionary process not helped along by an outside and guiding force—is highly improbable.

The design of our bodies and the complex interrelationships that exist in our universe beg for a Designer. The alternative is to say that time plus chance in the context of chaos created a universe of incredible order and creatures of stunning design. That's a hard sell.

In fact, it was precisely this line of reasoning that led Antony Flew, the Oxford philosophy professor who wrote the quintessential articles in favor of atheism for college philosophy textbooks the world over, to renounce his atheism. This is of personal interest to me because I studied at Oxford, and Antony Flew was just legendary.

And I don't know if you remember this, but if you take your old college philosophy textbooks, when you go to the "God section," they would have one writer giving you a reason to believe in God and then another article telling you why you shouldn't believe in God. Almost always the article written about why you shouldn't believe in God was written by Antony Flew from Oxford.

Well, he renounced his atheism because of what we just talked about. Here's an interview where he talked about it.

—————

Antony Flew Interview
https://youtu.be/mcFLnKk0o2E

—————

Related to all this is something called the anthropic principle, from the Greek word *anthropos*, which means "man" or "human."

Our world is uniquely suited to human beings and carbon-based life, the only form of life known to science. The argument is that as there are so many wonderful details that if changed even slightly would make it impossible for us to exist, then one is compelled to consider that somehow it was intentionally created for that very purpose.

Even Stephen Hawking, arguably the most brilliant physicist since Albert Einstein, wrote:

> It would be very difficult to explain why the universe should have begun in just this way, except as the act of a God who intended to create beings like us.[4]

Take a look at this video at how this plays out from a scientific perspective.

Anthropic Principle from "Case for a Creator"
https://youtu.be/xzwFQkwyCK0
begin at :53 into the clip

IV. The Humanness of Humans

So you have cause and effect, design and order. But there's another reason to believe, and it's what you know best: You.

Where does human personality come from? It's difficult for many to believe that the human personality—the soul, if you will—evolved out of a pool of primordial slime. Legs and arms and lungs, maybe—but what is inside of us? That which makes you, *you*? Consciousness itself?

When the philosopher René Descartes attempted to boil down his one and only true starting point for reflection, he came up with his famed phrase *cogito ergo sum*. I think, therefore, I am.

But where does that "thinking" come from? How are we able to think, reflect, feel, and reason? There is a voice inside of my head, a personality, a living spirit that I know exists and that is tangible and real when I think to myself. What is that, and where did it come from?

And that includes our spirituality. Because we are, all of us, deeply spiritual beings. One of the most interesting manifestations throughout all civilizations is the deep spiritual hunger of men and women. Anthropologists have discovered that human beings are incurably spiritual and conscious of the idea of God.

This was described by Blaise Pascal, the great seventeenth-century philosopher and mathematician, as the "God-shaped vacuum" in every human being. If there isn't a God, and we evolved naturalistically, that would not make sense.

In reflecting on this, C. S. Lewis noted that drives supposedly come about due to the realities of our world. For example, we have an appetite for food, and there is food to satisfy that need. The idea of naturalistic evolution is that our drives developed out of our bodies' needs and from the realities of the world.

We have this drive to know God, an authentic spiritual hunger, but there is no God? That doesn't make sense. If it were true, we shouldn't have the drive. Why would creatures who evolved by chance as a result of naturalistic causes alone desire and hunger after a Creator God?

Some have suggested that the answer to this is not God at all but a so-called God gene that has been hardwired into our genetic constitutions. But why would a gene like that have ever evolved?

Some take another tack and say the reason we're so spiritually hungry is simply our desire, our hope for a God. This was the belief of Sigmund Freud, the father of the psychoanalytic school of psychology.

The dilemma is that it doesn't explain the universal desire for God throughout time and across civilization. At some point, particularly in our modern context, you would think that the wish, desire, or need for God would simply end. Yet it only grows. In fact, just this past week (you may have seen it) the results came out from a twelve-year Pew research study that was charting out the future of world religion from 2010 to 2050. The headline was that we're going to be even more religious than ever. Religion is going to keep ascending. Which makes no evolutionary sense if there is no God.

But then there's the Bible's answer. We're spiritual because we were made to be. We were created by God and for God. Or as the biblical writer of Ecclesiastes put it, God has "set eternity in the human heart" (3:11).

Conclusion

So now it's your turn.

This was a lot to take in in a short amount of time, and we only just skimmed the surface.

Does the existence of God make more sense than the nonexistence of God?

You can say that the Big Bang banged itself.

You can say that the complexity and design of the universe, not to mention our bodies, came about through chance.

You can say our innate spirituality is just a fluke.

Or you can say, "Man, I'm having to work really hard to keep God out of this. Maybe it makes more sense to put him back into the equation. Because he seems to answer more questions than any other factor. Maybe all of this stuff thunders out the very reality of God."

And if you were with us last week, not just any God but the God who came in the person of Jesus. A God who wants to be known.

Let's stand for a closing prayer.

Notes

Chapter 1 A Seventh Age, the Second Fall, and the Rise of the Nones

1. Christopher Dawson, "The Six Ages of the Church," in *Christianity and European Culture*, ed. Gerald J. Russello (Washington, DC: Catholic University of America Press, 1998), 34–45.

2. Doug Sosnik, "America's Hinge Moment," *Politico*, March 29, 2015, http://www.politico.com/magazine/story/2015/03/2016-predictions-americas-sosnik-clinton-116480.

3. Philip Jenkins, *The Next Christendom: The Coming of Global Christianity* (Oxford: Oxford University Press, 2002), 126–27.

4. Samuel P. Huntington, *The Clash of Civilizations and the Remaking of World Order* (New York: Simon & Schuster, 1996).

5. James Gallagher, "UK Approves Three-Person Babies," BBC, February 24, 2015, http://www.bbc.com/news/health-31594856.

6. Peter L. Berger, ed., *The Desecularization of the World: Resurgent Religion and World Politics* (Washington, DC: Ethics and Public Policy Center; Grand Rapids: Eerdmans, 1999), 2.

7. Cathy Lynn Grossman, "'Nones' Now 15% of Population," *USA Today*, March 9, 2009, http://usatoday30.usatoday.com/news/religion/2009-03-09-aris-survey-nones_N.htm.

8. James Emery White, *The Rise of the Nones: Understanding and Reaching the Religiously Unaffiliated* (Grand Rapids: Baker Books, 2014), 16–17.

9. The Pew study still maintains that, instead of a single entity, such as the Southern Baptist Convention, evangelical Protestants are the largest group, but they do it by pooling together several groups and organizations.

10. Cathy Lynn Grossman, "Christians Lose Ground, 'Nones' Soar in New Portrait of US Religion," Religion News Service, May 12, 2015, http://www.religionnews.com/2015/05/12/christians-lose-ground-nones-soar-new-portrait-u-s-religion/.

11. "America's Changing Religious Landscape," Pew Research Center, May 12, 2015, http://www.pewforum.org/2015/05/12/americas-changing-religious-land

scape/; Grossman, "Christians Lose Ground"; Sarah Pulliam Bailey, "Christianity Faces Sharp Decline as Americans Are Becoming Even Less Affiliated with Religion," *Washington Post*, May 12, 2015, https://www.washingtonpost.com/news/acts-of-faith/wp/2015/05/12/christianity-faces-sharp-decline-as-americans-are-becoming-even-less-affiliated-with-religion/; and Nate Cohn, "Big Drop in Share of Americans Calling Themselves Christian," *New York Times*, May 12, 2015, http://www.nytimes.com/2015/05/12/upshot/big-drop-in-share-of-americans-calling-themselves-christian.html.

12. The emergence and definition of Generation Z are so new that some studies refer to them as "younger Millennials." But as will be detailed in the next chapter, they are best described as Generation Z.

13. "US Public Becoming Less Religious," Pew Research Center, November 3, 2015, http://www.pewforum.org/2015/11/03/u-s-public-becoming-less-religious/.

14. "2015 Sees Sharp Rise in Post-Christian Population," Barna Group, August 12, 2015, https://www.barna.org/barna-update/culture/728-america-more-post-christian-than-two-years-ago.

15. "Five Trends among the Unchurched," Barna Group, October 9, 2014, https://www.barna.org/barna-update/culture/685-five-trends-among-the-unchurched.

16. Tobin Grant, "Graphs: 5 Signs of the 'Great Decline' of Religion in America," Religion News Service, August 1, 2014, http://tobingrant.religionnews.com/2014/08/01/five-signs-great-decline-religion-america-gallup-graphs-church/.

17. Ruth Gledhill, "Exclusive: New Figures Reveal Massive Decline in Religious Affiliation," *Christian Today*, October 17, 2014, http://www.christiantoday.com/article/exclusive.new.figures.reveal.massive.decline.in.religious.affiliation/41799.htm.

18. John Bingham and Steven Swinford, "Britain Is No Longer a Christian Country and Should Stop Acting as If It Is, Says Judge," *Telegraph*, December 7, 2015, http://www.telegraph.co.uk/education/12036287/Britain-is-no-longer-a-Christian-country-and-should-stop-acting-as-if-it-is-says-judge.html.

19. "America's Changing Religious Landscape."

20. Peter L. Berger, *The Sacred Canopy: Elements of a Sociological Theory of Religion* (New York: Anchor Books, 1967), 107. See also David Martin, *A General Theory of Secularization* (Oxford: Blackwell, 1978); and Martin E. Marty, *The Modern Schism* (London: SCM, 1969).

21. Os Guinness, *The Gravedigger File: Papers on the Subversion of the Modern Church* (Downers Grove, IL: InterVarsity, 1983), 74. Cf. Thomas Luckmann, *The Invisible Religion* (New York: Macmillan, 1967). Perhaps the best investigation into this dynamic of modernity was offered by Robert Bellah et al., *Habits of the Heart: Individualism and Commitment in American Life* (San Francisco: Harper & Row, 1985). A chronicle of America's privatization of faith can be found in Phillip L. Berman, *The Search for Meaning: Americans Talk about What They Believe and Why* (New York: Ballantine, 1990).

22. Berger, *Sacred Canopy*, 127. The historical background to this stream of modernity is charted in Nathan O. Hatch, *The Democratization of American Christianity* (New Haven: Yale University Press, 1989).

23. Guinness, *Gravedigger File*, 93.

24. Berger, *Sacred Canopy*, 127. The idea of religion as a canopy serves as the motif for Martin E. Marty's exploration of modern American religion. See *Modern American Religion*, vol. 1, *The Irony of It All, 1893–1919* (Chicago: University of Chicago Press, 1986), the first of several volumes on twentieth-century American religion.

25. "US Public Becoming Less Religious."

26. Patrick Foster, "God Banished from *Downton Abbey*, Says Show's Historical Advisor," *Telegraph*, November 15, 2015, http://www.telegraph.co.uk/news/media/11997169/God-banished-from-Downton-Abbey-says-shows-historical-advisor.html.

27. Ed Stetzer, "Religious Polarization on the Way," *USA Today*, November 12, 2015, http://www.usatoday.com/story/opinion/2015/11/08/religion-secular-none-pew-research-protestant-column/75115070/.

Chapter 2 Meet Generation Z

1. "The Mindset List: 2019 List," Beloit College, https://www.beloit.edu/mindset/2019/.

2. Jill Novak, "The Six Living Generations in America," Marketing Teacher, http://www.marketingteacher.com/the-six-living-generations-in-america/.

3. Leonid Bershidsky, "Here Comes Generation Z," *Bloomberg View*, June 18, 2014, http://www.bloombergview.com/articles/2014-06-18/nailing-generation-z.

4. Jeremy Finch, "What Is Generation Z, and What Does It Want?," *Fast Company*, May 4, 2015, http://www.fastcoexist.com/3045317/what-is-generation-z-and-what-does-it-want.

5. "Meet Generation Z: The Second Generation within the Giant 'Millennial' Cohort," Bruce Tulgan and RainmakerThinking, 2013, http://rainmakerthinking.com/assets/uploads/2013/10/Gen-Z-Whitepaper.pdf.

6. David Pakman, "May I Have Your Attention, Please?," Medium.com, August 10, 2015, https://medium.com/life-learning/may-i-have-your-attention-please-19ef6395b2c3.

7. Alex Williams, "Move Over Millennials: Here Comes Generation Z," *New York Times*, September 20, 2015, http://www.nytimes.com/2015/09/20/fashion/move-over-millennials-here-comes-generation-z.html.

8. Sparks and Honey Culture Forecast, "Gen Z 2025: The Final Generation," 2016, 89, https://reports.sparksandhoney.com/campaign/generation-z-2025-the-final-generation.

9. Williams, "Move Over Millennials."

10. Sam Sanders, "Why Do Young People Like Socialism More Than Older People?" National Public Radio, November 21, 2015, http://www.npr.org/2015/11/21/456676215/why-do-young-people-like-socialism-more-than-older-people.

11. "Meet Generation Z: Forget Everything You Learned about Millennials," Sparks and Honey, June 17, 2014, http://www.slideshare.net/sparksandhoney/generation-z-final-june-17.

12. Cathy Lynn Grossman, "Americans Fret about Islam, Immigrants, the Future—and Each Other," Religion News Service, November 17, 2015, http://www.religionnews.com/2015/11/17/islam-terrorism-black-lives-matter/.

13. "Meet Generation Z," Sparks and Honey.

14. "Innovation Imperative: Meet Generation Z," Northeastern University, http://www.northeastern.edu/news/2014/11/innovation-imperative-meet-generation-z/.

15. Alexandra Levit, "Make Way for Generation Z," *New York Times*, March 20, 2015, http://www.nytimes.com/2015/03/29/jobs/make-way-for-generation-z.html?_r=0.

16. "Meet Generation Z," Sparks and Honey.

17. David Sims, "All Hail 'The Founders,'" *Atlantic*, December 2, 2015, http://www.theatlantic.com/entertainment/archive/2015/12/all-hail-the-founders/418458/.

18. Logan LaPlante, "Hackschooling Makes Me Happy," TEDx, University of Nevada, https://www.youtube.com/watch?v=h11u3vtcpaY.

19. "'Millennials on Steroids': Is Your Brand Ready for Generation Z?," Knowledge@Wharton, September 28, 2015, http://knowledge.wharton.upenn.edu/article/millennials-on-steroids-is-your-brand-ready-for-generation-z/.

20. William J. Bernstein, *Masters of the Word: How Media Shaped History from the Alphabet to the Internet* (New York: Grove Press, 2013), 5.

21. Ibid., 12.

22. David Bauder, "Teens Spend an Average of 9 Hours a Day with Media," Associated Press, November 3, 2015, http://abcnews.go.com/Entertainment/wireStory/teens-spend-average-hours-day-media-34927412.

23. Sparks and Honey Culture Forecast, "Gen Z 2025," 30.

24. "'Millennials on Steroids.'"

25. Nathan Ingraham, "Apple Announces 1 Million Apps in the App Store, More than 1 Billion Songs Played on iTunes Radio," The Verge, October 22, 2013, http://www.theverge.com/2013/10/22/4866302/apple-announces-1-million-apps-in-the-app-store.

26. Brian X. Chen, *Always On: How the iPhone Unlocked the Anything-Anytime-Anywhere Future—and Locked Us In* (Boston: Da Capo Press, 2011).

27. Amanda Lenhart, "Teens, Social Media, and Technology Overview 2015," Pew Research Center, April 9, 2015, http://www.pewinternet.org/2015/04/09/teens-social-media-technology-2015/.

28. Sparks and Honey Culture Forecast, "Gen Z 2025," 25.

29. Cooper Smith, "'Generation Z' Is Poised to Drive a Surge in E-Commerce Growth," *Business Insider*, January 26, 2015, http://www.businessinsider.com/generation-z-e-commerce-shopping-2014-9.

30. Nisha Lilia Diu, "Look Out, Generation Z Is about to Enter Your Workplace," *Telegraph*, July 19, 2015, http://www.telegraph.co.uk/education/universityeducation/11746954/Look-out-Generation-Z-is-about-to-enter-your-workplace.html.

31. Quentin J. Schultze, *Habits of the High-Tech Heart* (Grand Rapids: Baker, 2002), 21.

32. Gary D. Myers, "Theological Ed. Is 'Being Redefined,'" Baptist Press, April 20, 2011, http://www.bpnews.net/bpnews.asp?id=35098.

33. Sparks and Honey Culture Forecast, "Gen Z 2025," 56.

34. Finch, "What Is Generation Z, and What Does It Want?"

35. "'Millennials on Steroids.'"

36. "Innovation Imperative."

37. "Meet Generation Z," Sparks and Honey.

38. "Innovation Imperative"; see also the Pew Research Center study, "Teens, Technology, and Romantic Relationships," released October 1, 2015, http://www.pewinternet.org/2015/10/01/teens-technology-and-romantic-relationships/.

39. Doug Sosnik, "America's Hinge Moment," *Politico*, March 29, 2015, http://www.politico.com/magazine/story/2015/03/2016-predictions-americas-sosnik-clinton-116480.

40. Novak, "The Six Living Generations in America."

41. Williams, "Move Over Millennials."

42. "Meet Generation Z," Sparks and Honey.

43. "New Census Bureau Report Analyzes US Population Projections," Census.gov, March 3, 2015, http://www.census.gov/newsroom/press-releases/2015/cb15-tps16.html.

44. Leonid Bershidsky, "Generation Z Pushing Back against Today's Technology," Bloomberg News, November 19, 2014, http://www.charlotteobserver.com/opinion/op-ed/article9233846.html.

45. "Meet Generation Z," Sparks and Honey.

46. Sparks and Honey Culture Forecast, "Gen Z 2025," 46.

47. "Innovation Imperative."

48. Michael Gerson and Peter Wehner, "How Christians Can Flourish in a Same-Sex-Marriage World," *Christianity Today*, November 2, 2015, http://www.christianitytoday.com/ct/2015/november/how-christians-can-flourish-in-same-sex-marriage-world-cult.html.

49. Eric Sasson, "Kristen Stewart, Miley Cyrus, and the Rise of Sexual Fluidity," *Wall Street Journal*, August 17, 2015, http://blogs.wsj.com/speakeasy/2015/08/17/kristen-stewart-miley-cyrus-and-the-rise-of-sexual-fluidity/.

50. Helena Horton, "Nearly Half of Young People Don't Think They Are Heterosexual," *Telegraph*, August 17, 2015, http://www.telegraph.co.uk/news/uk news/11807740/half-young-people-heterosexual-lgbt-homosexual-yougov.html.

51. "Meet Generation Z," Sparks and Honey.

52. "Innovation Imperative."

53. David Freed and Idrees Kahloon, "Beliefs and Lifestyle," *Harvard Crimson*, http://features.thecrimson.com/2015/freshman-survey/lifestyle/.

54. "US Public Becoming Less Religious," Pew Research Center, November 3, 2015, http://www.pewforum.org/2015/11/03/u-s-public-becoming-less-religious/.

55. "Five Trends among the Unchurched," Barna Group, October 9, 2014, https://www.barna.org/barna-update/culture/685-five-trends-among-the-unchurched.

Chapter 3 When Christ and His Saints Slept

1. "Meet Generation Z: Forget Everything You Learned about Millennials," Sparks and Honey, June 17, 2014, http://www.slideshare.net/sparksandhoney/generation-z-final-june-17.

2. Lenore Skenazy, "Why I Let My 9-Year-Old Ride the Subway Alone," *New York Sun*, April 1, 2008, http://www.nysun.com/news/why-i-let-my-9-year-old-ride-subway-alone.

3. Harry Wallop, "We Can't Switch Off a Child's Online World," *Telegraph*, January 19, 2014, http://www.telegraph.co.uk/technology/internet/10583072/We-cant-switch-off-a-childs-online-world.html.

4. Tamar Lewin, "If Your Kids Are Awake, They're Probably Online," *New York Times*, January 20, 2010, http://www.nytimes.com/2010/01/20/education/20wired.html.

5. Neil Postman, *The Disappearance of Childhood* (New York: Delacorte Press, 1982).

6. Graeme Paton, "Children Losing a Love of Stories in the Digital Age, Warns Head," *Daily Telegraph*, July 25, 2013, 11; and Rhys Blakely, "Game Is Up for Traditional Pastimes with Half-Hour Version of Monopoly," *Times* (London), July 26, 2013, 7.

7. The following is adapted from James Emery White, *The Church in an Age of Crisis* (Grand Rapids: Baker Books, 2012), 124–25.

8. Pamela Paul, "The Playground Gets Even Tougher," *New York Times*, October 8, 2010, http://www.nytimes.com/2010/10/10/fashion/10Cultural.html.

9. Ibid.

10. Marshall McLuhan with Quentin Fiore, *The Medium Is the Massage: An Inventory of Effects* (Corte Madera, CA: Gingko Press, 1967/2001), 26.

11. Fred Fedler, *An Introduction to the Mass Media* (Australia: Harcourt Publishers, 1978), 7.

12. "MTV Is Rock around the Clock," *Philadelphia Inquirer*, November 3, 1982, D-1, D-4.

13. Holly Finn, "Online Pornography's Effects, and a New Way to Fight Them," *Wall Street Journal*, May 3, 2013, http://www.wsj.com/articles/SB100014241278 87323628004578456710204395042.

14. Niamh Horan, "Porn Now the Wallpaper of Our Lives," Independent.ie, October 18, 2015, http://www.independent.ie/entertainment/porn-now-the-wall paper-of-our-lives-34118532.html.

15. Ann Olivarius, "Revenge Porn Is Not Part of 'Everyday Life': Something Has Gone Terribly Wrong with Our Teens," *Telegraph*, December 7, 2015, http://www.telegraph.co.uk/women/sex/revenge-porn-is-not-part-of-everyday-life-something-has-gone-ter/. For the 2015 report, see http://www.paconsulting.com/our-thinking/cybercrime-2015/.

16. Ross O'Hara, "Exposure to Sexual Content in Popular Movies Predicts Sexual Behavior in Adolescence," *Psychological Science*, July 17, 2012, http://www.psychologicalscience.org/index.php/news/releases/exposure-to-sexual-content-in-popular-movies-predicts-sexual-behavior-in-adolescence.html.

17. Carolyn C. Ross, MD, MPH, "Overexposed and Under-Prepared: The Effects of Early Exposure to Sexual Content," *Psychology Today*, August 13, 2012, https://www.psychologytoday.com/blog/real-healing/201208/overexposed-and-under-prepared-the-effects-early-exposure-sexual-content.

18. Eric Schmidt and Jared Cohen, *The New Digital Age: Reshaping the Future of People, Nations, and Business* (New York: Alfred A. Knopf, 2013), 3.

19. Nisha Lilia Diu, "Look Out, Generation Z Is about to Enter Your Workplace," *Telegraph*, July 19, 2015, http://www.telegraph.co.uk/education/university

education/11746954/Look-out-Generation-Z-is-about-to-enter-your-work place.html.

20. Miranda Prynne, "'Sexting Is New Courtship,' Parents Are Told," *Telegraph*, May 5, 2014, http://www.telegraph.co.uk/technology/10808862/Sexting-is -new-courtship-parents-are-told.html.

21. Pamela Paul, *Pornified* (New York: Times Books, 2005), second cover.

22. The following is adapted from James Emery White, *What They Didn't Teach You in Seminary* (Grand Rapids: Baker Books, 2011), 55–56.

23. Finn, "Online Pornography's Effects, and a New Way to Fight Them."

24. Ibid.

25. Rod Dreher, "The Porn Catastrophe," *American Conservative*, April 5, 2016, http://www.theamericanconservative.com/dreher/the-porn-catastrophe/.

26. Ruth Graham, "Why Hold a Child Hostage to My Doubts," *Slate*, http://www.slate.com/articles/life/faithbased/2015/11/nones_who_raise_their_kids _with_religion_in_losing_our_religion_how_unaffiliated.html.

27. Cathy Lynn Grossman, "As Protestants Decline, Those with No Religion Gain," *USA Today*, October 9, 2012, http://www.usatoday.com/story/news/nation /2012/10/08/nones-protestant-religion-pew/1618445/.

28. Dan Merica, "Survey: One in Five Americans Has No Religion," CNN, October 9, 2012, http://religion.blogs.cnn.com/2012/10/09/survey-one-in-five -americans-is-religiously-unaffiliated/.

29. Graham, "Why Hold a Child Hostage to My Doubts."

30. Malasree Home, *The Peterborough Version of the Anglo-Saxon Chronicle: Rewriting Post-conquest History* (Woodbridge, Suffolk: The Boydell Press, 2015), 88.

31. Stephen Prothero, *Religious Literacy: What Every American Needs to Know* (San Francisco: HarperSanFrancisco, 2007), 293–94.

Chapter 4 The Countercultural Church

1. John R. W. Stott, *Christian Counter-Culture: The Message of the Sermon on the Mount* (Downers Grove, IL: InterVarsity, 1978), 10.

2. The following is taken from James Emery White, *Christ Among the Dragons* (Downers Grove, IL: InterVarsity Press, 2010), 136–38.

3. This introduction to the church is taken from ibid., 144–47.

4. These marks were affirmed in both the Nicene (AD 325) and the Niceno-Constantinopolitan (AD 381) Creeds.

5. Jürgen Moltmann, *The Church in the Power of the Spirit* (New York: Harper & Row, 1977), 10. See also Darrell L. Guder, ed., *Missional Church: A Vision for the Sending of the Church in North America* (Grand Rapids: Eerdmans, 1998).

6. Christopher J. H. Wright, *The Mission of God: Unlocking the Bible's Grand Narrative* (Downers Grove, IL: InterVarsity, 2006), 22–23.

7. "US Public Becoming Less Religious," Pew Research Center, November 3, 2015, http://www.pewforum.org/2015/11/03/u-s-public-becoming-less-religious/.

8. Martin E. Marty sounds this theme in *Modern American Religion*, vol. 1, *The Irony of It All, 1893–1919* (Chicago: University of Chicago Press, 1986), noting that the fundamentalist movement was decisively "countermodern" (see

chapters 10 and 11). See also H. Richard Niebuhr, *Christ and Culture* (New York: Harper, 1951), 45–82.

9. George Marsden, *Fundamentalism and American Culture: The Shaping of Twentieth Century Evangelicalism, 1870–1925* (Oxford: Oxford University Press, 1980), 194.

10. Quoted in Ray H. Abrams, *Preachers Present Arms* (New York: Herald Press, 1969), 79, as quoted in Marsden, *Fundamentalism*, 142.

11. Marsden, *Fundamentalism*, 149.

12. Thomas S. Kuhn, *The Structure of Scientific Revolutions*, 2nd ed. (Chicago: University of Chicago Press, 1962, 1970).

13. Marsden, *Fundamentalism*, 215.

14. On this, see Bruce L. Shelley, "Evangelicalism," in *Dictionary of Christianity in America*, ed. Daniel G. Reid (Downers Grove, IL: InterVarsity, 1990).

15. Kenneth Woodward, "Born Again: The Year of the Evangelical," *Newsweek*, October 25, 1976.

16. Obviously, concern with secular humanism was not without warrant. The American Humanist Association set forth *The Humanist Manifesto I* and *The Humanist Manifesto II*, ed. Paul Kurtz (Amherst, NY: Prometheus, 1973), which clearly set forth their disbelief in God yet total enthusiasm for humanity.

17. This idea was popularized widely by Peter Marshall and David Manuel in *The Light and the Glory* (Grand Rapids: Revell, 1977). A team of evangelical historians attempted to lay this theory to rest, but it is far from diminished as a popular framework for viewing American history. See Mark Noll, Nathan Hatch, and George Marsden, *The Search for Christian America* (Colorado Springs: Helmers & Howard, 1989).

18. David Brooks, "The Next Culture War," *New York Times*, June 30, 2015, http://www.nytimes.com/2015/06/30/opinion/david-brooks-the-next-culture-war.html.

19. Clifford Geertz, *The Interpretation of Cultures: Selected Essays by Clifford Geertz* (New York: Basic Books, 1973), 5. See especially the opening chapter, "Thick Description: Toward an Interpretive Theory of Culture," 3–30.

20. Sword & Spoon Group, http://www.swordandspoongroup.com/our-partners/.

21. Michael Gerson and Peter Wehner, "How Christians Can Flourish in a Same-Sex-Marriage World," *Christianity Today*, November 2, 2015, http://www.christianitytoday.com/ct/2015/november/how-christians-can-flourish-in-same-sex-marriage-world-cult.html?.

22. Quoted in ibid.

23. Ibid.

24. Quoted in ibid. Also see Rodney Stark, *The Triumph of Christianity: How the Jesus Movement Became the World's Largest Religion* (New York: HarperCollins, 2011).

25. Rod Dreher, "Coming to Terms with a Post-Christian World," *Christianity Today*, November 2, 2015, http://www.christianitytoday.com/ct/2015/november/coming-to-terms-with-post-christian-world.html, in response to Michael Gerson and Peter Wehner, "The Power of Our Weakness," *Christianity Today*, November 2015, 48.

26. As quoted by William Rees-Mogg in *Times* (London), April 4, 2005, http://en .wikiquote.org/wiki/Mahatma_Gandhi.

27. Michael Green, *Evangelism in the Early Church* (United Kingdom: Hodder & Stoughton, 1970), 173.

28. *Apology of Tertullian*, AD 197, http://www.tertullian.org/articles/reeve _apology.htm.

29. The Minchin video can be found at http://www.youtube.com/watch? v=r0xQcEH7Dqo. See also Dan Savage, "What God Wants," *New York Times Book Review*, April 14, 2013.

30. David Kinnaman and Gabe Lyons, *UnChristian: What a New Generation Really Thinks about Christianity* (Grand Rapids: Baker, 2007), 28. See also David Van Biema, "Christianity's Image Problem," Time.com, October 2, 2007, http:// content.time.com/time/nation/article/0,8599,1667639,00.html.

31. Study performed in 1992 by the Barna Research Group, Glendale, California. First published in James Emery White, *Rethinking the Church* (Grand Rapids: Baker Books, 1997), 23.

32. Thomas Cahill, *How the Irish Saved Civilization* (New York: Anchor Books, 1995), 3.

33. Ibid., 193–94.

34. Alister McGrath, *The Twilight of Atheism* (New York: Doubleday, 2004), xi.

35. On this, see James Emery White, *A Mind for God* (Downers Grove, IL: InterVarsity, 2006), 13.

Chapter 5 Finding Our Voice

1. Jonathan Merritt, "Hillsong's Brian Houston Says Church Won't Take Public Position on LGBT Issues," Religion News Service, October 16, 2014, http:// jonathanmerritt.religionnews.com/2014/10/16/hillsongs-brian-houston-says -church-lgbt-issues.

2. Ibid.

3. Nicola Menzie, "Hillsong's Brian Houston on Gay Marriage: 'I Believe the Writings of Paul Are Clear on This Subject,'" *The Christian Post*, October 18, 2014, http://www.christianpost.com/news/hillsongs-brian-houston -on-gay-marriage-i-believe-the-writings-of-paul-are-clear-on-this-subject -128282/.

4. Merritt, "Hillsong's Brian Houston Says Church Won't Take Public Position on LGBT Issues."

5. John R. W. Stott, *Between Two Worlds: The Art of Preaching in the Twentieth Century* (Grand Rapids: Eerdmans, 1982), 89.

6. Carol Kuruvilla, "Former Megachurch Pastor Rob Bell: A Church That Doesn't Support Gay Marriage Is 'Irrelevant,'" *Huffington Post*, February 20, 2015, http://www.huffingtonpost.com/2015/02/20/rob-bell-oprah-gay-marriage_n _6723840.html.

7. Millard Erickson, *Christian Theology*, 2nd ed. (Grand Rapids: Baker, 1983, 1998, 2007), 123–29.

8. Stott, *Between Two Worlds*.

9. Christopher J. H. Wright, *An Eye for an Eye: The Place of Old Testament Ethics Today* (Downers Grove, IL: InterVarsity, 1983), 187.

10. Mark Galli, "The New Battle for the Bible," *Christianity Today*, October 2015, 33.

11. Greg Lukianoff and Jonathan Haidt, "The Coddling of the American Mind," *Atlantic*, September 2016, http://www.theatlantic.com/magazine/archive /2015/09/the-coddling-of-the-american-mind/399356/.

12. Ibid.

13. Ibid.

14. Ibid.

15. Sharon Shahid, "If MLK Had Tweeted from Jail," *USA Today*, January 12, 2011, http://www.usatoday.com/news/opinion/forum/2011-01-05-column12 _ST_N.htm.

16. Gene Edward Veith, "Reading and Writing Worldviews," in *The Christian Imagination: The Practice of Faith in Literature and Writing*, ed. Leland Ryken, rev. and exp. ed. (Colorado Springs: Shaw, 2002), 119.

17. Jonathan Edwards, "Notes on the Mind," in *The Works of Jonathan Edwards: Scientific and Philosophical Writings*, ed. Wallace E. Anderson (New Haven: Yale University Press, 1980), cclxvii.

18. Charles Colson and Nancy Pearcey, *How Now Shall We Live?* (Wheaton: Tyndale, 1999).

19. Martin Luther King Jr., *Why We Can't Wait (Letter from a Birmingham Jail)* (New York: Mentor/New American Library, 1963, 1964), 93.

Chapter 6 Rethinking Evangelism

1. The following is adapted from James Emery White, *The Rise of the Nones* (Grand Rapids: Baker Books, 2014), 90–93.

2. C. S. Lewis, "Modern Man and His Categories of Thought," in *Present Concerns* (London: Fount Paperbacks, 1986), 66.

3. *Gravity*, directed by Alfonso Cuarón (Burbank, CA: Warner Bros., 2013).

4. Chip Heath and Dan Heath, *Made to Stick: Why Some Ideas Survive and Others Die* (New York: Random House, 2007), 19–21.

5. See the National Center for Biotechnology Information and the US National Library of Medicine, as reported by the Statistic Brain Research Institute: http:// www.statisticbrain.com/attention-span-statistics/.

6. Harald Weinreich, Hartmut Obendorf, Eelco Herder, and Matthias Mayer, "Not Quite the Average: An Empirical Study of Web Use," in the ACM Transactions on the Web 2, no. 1 (February 2008), art. 5.

7. "Meet Generation Z: Forget Everything You Learned about Millennials," Sparks and Honey, June 17, 2014, http://www.slideshare.net/sparksandhoney /generation-z-final-june-17.

8. Jeremy Finch, "What Is Generation Z, and What Does It Want?," *Fast Company*, May 4, 2015, http://www.fastcoexist.com/3045317/what-is-generation -z-and-what-does-it-want.

9. Alex Williams, "Move Over Millennials: Here Comes Generation Z," *New York Times*, September 20, 2015, http://www.nytimes.com/2015/09/20/fashion /move-over-millennials-here-comes-generation-z.html.

10. Kevin Clark, "How the Rams Built a Laboratory for Millennials," *Wall Street Journal*, September 14, 2015, http://www.wsj.com/articles/how-the-rams -built-a-laboratory-for-millennials-1442257224.

11. Alex Williams, "Move Over Millennials: Here Comes Generation Z," *New York Times*, September 20, 2015, http://www.nytimes.com/2015/09/20/fashion /move-over-millennials-here-comes-generation-z.html.

12. The following is adapted from James Emery White, *The Rise of the Nones* (Grand Rapids: Baker Books, 2014), 160–63.

13. Flavia Di Consiglio, "Lindisfarne Gospels: Why Is This Book So Special?" BBC Religion and Ethics, March 20, 2013, http://www.bbc.co.uk/religion/0/21 588667.

14. "Oxford Dictionaries Word of the Year 2015 Is . . . ," Oxford Dictionaries Blog, November 16, 2015, http://blog.oxforddictionaries.com/2015/11/word-of -the-year-2015-emoji/. See also Hannah Furness, "Oxford Dictionary Swaps Word of the Year for Public's Favorite Emoji," *Telegraph*, November 17, 2015, http://www .telegraph.co.uk/news/newstopics/howaboutthat/11999230/Oxford-Dictionary -swaps-Word-of-the-Year-for-publics-favourite-emoji.html.

15. "Meet Generation Z," Sparks and Honey.

16. "Five Trends among the Unchurched," Barna Group, October 9, 2014, https:// www.barna.org/barna-update/culture/685-five-trends-among-the-unchurched#.

17. Sparks and Honey Culture Forecast, "Gen Z 2025: The Final Genera- tion," 2016, 16, https://reports.sparksandhoney.com/campaign/generation-z-2025 -the-final-generation.

18. Ibid., 66.

19. Willard Foxton, "Strict Mistress? The World's Secret Sexual Preferences Re- vealed by Google," *Telegraph*, October 31, 2014, http://www.telegraph.co.uk/tech nology/google/11201009/Strict-Mistress-The-worlds-secret-sexual-preferences -revealed-by-Google.html.

20. Emma Green, "The Origins of Aggressive Atheism," *Atlantic*, Novem- ber, 2014, http://www.theatlantic.com/national/archive/2014/11/the-origins-of -aggressive-atheism/383088/.

21. "Meet Generation Z," Sparks and Honey.

22. Rukmini Callimachi, "ISIS and the Lonely Young American," *New York Times*, June 27, 2015, http://www.nytimes.com/2015/06/28/world/americas/isis -online-recruiting-american.html.

23. "US Public Becoming Less Religious," Pew Research Center, November 3, 2015, http://www.pewforum.org/2015/11/03/u-s-public-becoming-less-religious/.

24. John Bingham, "Talking about Christianity Could Just Put People Off— Church of England Signals," *Telegraph*, November 6, 2015, http://www.telegraph .co.uk/news/religion/11966960/Talking-about-Christianity-could-just-put-people -off-Church-of-England-signals.html.

Chapter 7 Apologetics for a New Generation

1. Andrew Higgins, "Norway Has a New Passion: Ghost Hunting," *New York Times*, October 24, 2015, http://www.nytimes.com/2015/10/25/world/europe/for -many-norwegians-ghosts-fill-a-void.html.

2. Pitirim Sorokin, *Social and Cultural Dynamics*, rev. ed. (New Brunswick, NJ: Transaction Publishers, 2010).

3. Christopher Dawson, *Dynamics of World History*, ed. John J. Mulloy (Wilmington, DE: ISI Books, 2002), 98.

4. "CBS Cancels '60 Minutes' Wed., 'Amy'—Jennifer Love Hewitt in New Series," CNN.com, May 18, 2005; Aimee Picchi/ Bloomberg News, "Networks Hoping Viewers Feel Lure of Supernatural (ABC, NBC, CBS Preview 5 New Shows Based on Paranormal)," *Charlotte Observer*, May 14, 2005, 4E; and "CBS Moonves: 'Ghosts Skew Better Than God,'" *Drudge Report*, May 19, 2005.

5. "The Charlie Charlie Challenge—What Is the Spooky Craze?," *Telegraph*, May 27, 2015, http://www.telegraph.co.uk/news/newstopics/howaboutthat/116 28862/Charlie-Charlie-Challenge-what-is-it-what-is-the-explanation.html.

6. The same could be said of the "hard to penetrate" Muslim world, where reports of deeply unsettling, realistic dreams of Jesus are driving Muslims to Christians for explanation.

7. "US Public Becoming Less Religious," Pew Research Center, November 3, 2015, http://www.pewforum.org/2015/11/03/u-s-public-becoming-less-religious/.

8. Lisa Cannon Green, "Study: Nonreligious Americans See Evidence of Creator," Baptist Press, October 7, 2015, http://www.bpnews.net/45612/study--non religious-americans-see-evidence-of-creator.

9. Traci Watson, "Gravitational Waves Offer New Insight into Big Bang," *USA Today*, March 18, 2014, http://www.usatoday.com/story/tech/2014/03/17 /big-bang-gravitational-waves/6520537/. See also Dennis Overbye, "Space Ripples Reveal Big Bang's Smoking Gun," *New York Times*, March 17, 2014, http://www .nytimes.com/2014/03/18/science/space/detection-of-waves-in-space-buttresses -landmark-theory-of-big-bang.html.

10. Alan Guth, *The Inflationary Universe* (New York: Perseus Books, 1997).

11. Ian Barbour, *When Science Meets Religion: Enemies, Strangers, or Partners?* (New York: HarperCollins, 2000), xi.

12. Carl Sagan, *The Demon-Haunted World: Science as a Candle in the Dark* (New York: Random House, 1996).

13. Adam Frank, "The Most Dangerous Ideas in Science," National Public Radio, January 27, 2015, http://www.npr.org/blogs/13.7/2015/01/27/381809832 /the-most-dangerous-ideas-in-science.

14. Robert Jastrow, *God and the Astronomers* (New York: Norton, 1978), 107.

Chapter 8 Decisions

1. The following is adapted from James Emery White, *What They Didn't Teach You in Seminary* (Grand Rapids: Baker Books, 2011), 75–76, 77–79.

2. The following is adapted from James Emery White, *The Rise of the Nones* (Grand Rapids, Baker Books, 2014), 76–77, 80–81, 83–84.

Afterword

1. *Webster's New World College Dictionary*, 4th ed., s.v. "aggressive."

Appendix A Gay Marriage

1. Editorial, "Just Married?," *Christianity Today*, April 24, 2000, http://www
.christianitytoday.com/ct/2000/april24/27.40.html.

2. Edith Humphrey, "What God Hath Not Joined," *Christianity Today*, September 1, 2004, http://www.christianitytoday.com/ct/2004/september/11.36.html.

Appendix B Map of the Spiritual World

1. Lee Speigel, "Spooky Number of Americans Believe in Ghosts," *Huffington
Post*, February 8, 2013, http://www.huffingtonpost.com/2013/02/02/real-ghosts
-americans-poll_n_2049485.html.

2. Billy Graham, *Angels: God's Secret Agents* (Nashville: Thomas Nelson,
1975), 3–4.

3. C. S. Lewis, *The Screwtape Letters* (New York: Bantam, 1982), 36.

Appendix C Why Believe in God?

1. "200 Movie Trivia Questions and Answers," BuzzKenya, http://buzzkenya
.com/movie-trivia-questions-answers/.

2. Mike Wall, "Major Discovery: 'Smoking Gun' for Universe's Incredible
Big Bang Expansion Found," Space.com, March 17, 2014, http://www.space
.com/25078-universe-inflation-gravitational-waves-discovery.html.

3. Fred Hoyle, *The Intelligent Universe* (London: Michael Joseph, 1983), 11–12.

4. Stephen Hawking, *A Brief History of Time* (New York: Bantam Books,
1988), 127.

James Emery White is the founding and senior pastor of Mecklenburg Community Church in Charlotte, North Carolina; the president of Serious Times, a ministry that explores the intersection of faith and culture and hosts ChurchAndCulture.org; a ranked adjunctive professor of theology and culture at Gordon-Conwell Theological Seminary, where he also served as its fourth president; and the author of more than twenty books that have been translated into ten languages.

Mecklenburg Community Church began with a single family and has grown to more than ten thousand active attendees across multiple campuses. Meck experiences over 70 percent of its growth from those who were previously unchurched, and during its formative years it was often cited as one of the fastest-growing church starts in the United States.

Dr. White holds a BS degree in public relations and business, along with MDiv and PhD degrees from Southern Seminary, where he was awarded a Garrett Teaching Fellowship in both New Testament and theology. He has also done advanced university study at Vanderbilt University in American religious history and continuing education at Oxford University in England, including participation in Oxford's Summer Programme in Theology.

Dr. White and his wife, Susan, have four children and three grandchildren.

ALSO BY
JAMES EMERY WHITE

LIKE THIS
BOOK?

Consider sharing it with others!

- Share or mention the book on your social media platforms. Use the hashtag **#MeetGenerationZ**.

- Write a book review on your blog or on a retailer site.

- Pick up a copy for friends, family, or strangers— anyone who you think would enjoy and be challenged by its message!

- Share this message on Twitter or Facebook: **"I loved #MeetGenerationZ by @JamesEmeryWhite // ChurchAndCulture.org @ReadBakerBooks"**

- Recommend this book for your church, workplace, book club, or class.

- Follow Baker Books on social media and tell us what you like.

 Facebook.com/ReadBakerBooks

 @ReadBakerBooks